Christopher Gower was born in I
time as an undergraduate readin
University, has always resided and worked in the capital. Prior
to ordination as an Anglican priest he was a civil servant and
for four years a police officer in the Metropolitan Police. Since
ordination in 1973 he has worked in seven parishes (five as
the parish priest) and for 20 of those years has also been in
secular employment in local government in various London
boroughs, including in chief officer posts in education, leisure
and community services. For the past ten years he has been Rector
of St Marylebone Parish Church in Central London, with its
healing and counselling centre and NHS medical practice in
the crypt. His role as Rector includes his acting as chaplain to
several renowned private hospitals within the world famous
Harley Street medical community. He is also Chairman of the
Nigerian Anglican Chaplaincy in the United Kingdom, which
is based at St Marylebone, and an Honorary Canon of St
John's Cathedral in the Diocese of Ilesa, Nigeria. He has an MA
in pastoral liturgy from Heythrop College, London University
and an MTh in preaching from the University of Wales. He
is the author of *Speaking of Healing*, published by SPCK and
also translated into Spanish as *Hablar De Sanación Ante El
Sufrimiento*, which explores how to preach about healing. He
is married with two children.

# SACRAMENTS OF HEALING

Christopher Gower

First published in Great Britain in 2007

Society for Promoting Christian Knowledge
36 Causton Street
London SW1P 4ST

*British Library Cataloguing-in-Publication Data*
A catalogue record for this book is available from the British Library

ISBN 978–0–281–05944–7

1 3 5 7 9 10 8 6 4 2

Typeset by Graphicraft Ltd, Hong Kong
Printed in Great Britain by Ashford Colour Press

Produced on paper from sustainable forests

# Contents

# Contents

# Preface

Why write a book entitled *Sacraments of Healing*? One of the reasons is to look at healing from the objective standpoint of the historical sacramental tradition of the Church, in order to provide a counterbalance to the more subjective approaches of individual preachers/healers, often in itinerant healing ministries, who increasingly dominate the Christian landscape, but who occasionally get the healing ministry of the Church a bad press.

Another desire is to help encourage Catholic Christians, both within the Church of England and in the wider universal Church, to rediscover the healing power of the sacraments and in so doing further the renewal of the Church within that tradition. I also hope that those on the fast-growing evangelical/charismatic wing of the Church may come to see the value of a sacramental approach to the healing ministry that is less dependent upon the charisma of the preacher and the emotion of a highly charged worship setting.

This book is aimed both at the professional clergy, to encourage them in the Church's ministry of healing, and also at those who are sick or wounded and who need to be on the receiving end of such ministry. This has given me a problem as to what style to adopt in writing, not only for the theologically literate but also for those who may have no specialist background. I have therefore chosen to deal with each sacrament in turn, first by tracing its history, theology and liturgy in what I hope is an accessible style for those not conversant with such background, and then applying each sacrament to pastoral situations in a more personal way. I did not want to write a purely technical handbook on the sacraments on the one hand, or a book full of healing stories divorced from theological considerations on the other, for there are many such books. Both perspectives are necessary, but need to be brought together to inform each other.

The book is laced with anecdotes and humour, for which I do not apologize. I note that the scientist Richard Dawkins in his latest diatribe against religion *The God Delusion* mixes serious intellectual argument with a more knockabout style punctuated, to use his words, with 'a little comic relief' from time to time. Interestingly, even an atheist like Dawkins is prepared to admit that healing through faith works in a few cases, even though he does not attribute it to a divine cause.

Finally, I hope this book will be of help to those Christians who are uncertain about the divine dimension in healing. I like the story of a conversation that once took place during a survey. The interviewer asked a resident, 'Do you believe in God?' 'Yes,' the individual replied. The interviewer continued, 'Do you believe in a God who can change the course of events on earth?' 'No,' replied the interviewee, 'just the ordinary one.'

Perhaps this book will help those who believe in the 'ordinary God', to see how God can sometimes work in extraordinary ways and make a difference to our lives in bringing healing and wholeness through sacramental channels of grace.

# 1

## *Introduction*

———◆◆◆———

### *Health*

Health is one of the most important considerations occupying modern society, as we search for the Holy Grail which offers the alluring elixir of a long and healthy life. We are encouraged in this search by advertisements that display perfect bodies to sell their products, and are surrounded by a plethora of vitamin pills and supplements, chains of health and fitness clubs and the like.

Life expectancy has increased dramatically over the last century or so. At the beginning of the twentieth century average life expectancy for men was 45 years and for women 50. By the commencement of this century it had risen to 76 for men and 80 for women. Much of this increase is as a result of advances in medical science and technology, and new drugs and surgical techniques are constantly being developed to combat physical disease. An army of counsellors and psychotherapists has also been assembled to deal with emotional *dis-ease* prevalent in today's pressurized society, for many of our present-day illnesses are stress-related. Indeed, there has been a 50 per cent increase in the use of anti-depressants over the past ten years, and one in four people will suffer mental health problems at some stage in their lives. On top of all this there is an ever-expanding range of complementary and alternative medicines and therapies available, though the effectiveness of many of these remains as yet unproven.

Diet has also become a major factor in maintaining health. We are constantly being reminded to eat at least five portions of fruit and vegetables a day (provided they have not been contaminated by pesticides), to drink plenty of water, eat less meat and more fish (until the world's stock of seafood runs out through overfishing), and avoid intake of foods containing high levels of saturated fats. Such is the pressure from consumers, government bodies and health organizations to promote healthy eating that food manufacturers are having to reduce the sugar, fat and salt contents in their products (the path to a hospital bed is indeed sprinkled with salt). Fast-food giants are also in a hurry to remove killer hydrogenated vegetable oils or transfats from their product ranges. More and more space on supermarket shelves is being given to organic products, and food and drink are being labelled in such a way that consumers can see which products offer their version of the *bread of life* and *cup of salvation*, because they are more conducive to maintaining a healthy lifestyle. These dietary considerations, together with regular exercise and deliverance from the sins of smoking and other harmful practices, have assisted in prolonging life.

Although average life expectancy is likely to increase further as a result of continued advances in medical knowledge, it is threatened by obesity among the younger generation. Recent statistics have shown that more than a quarter of children in English secondary schools are clinically obese. As a result we are in danger of raising a generation of people who have a shorter life expectancy than their parents. This obesity is happening against the backdrop of large parts of the world suffering from malnutrition and where mortality rates among the under-fives are more than one in four births in some places. It is being claimed, however, that there are now more obese people in the world than those who are starving.

Scientific research has shown that the genes we inherit provide us with the basic blueprint for life – and death. Research is increasingly showing that the time we spend in our mother's womb, those 266 days or so from conception to birth, is the time when much of what will happen during the decades ahead is determined. The future of our health is written in the womb.

Genetic engineering will also increasingly be on the modern health agenda, as medical scientists seek to eradicate major diseases at source. Using genetic screening, doctors will be able to start treating illnesses before they even appear. This paradigm shift in screening technology will mean that thousands of parents at risk of passing on inherited diseases and disabilities to their children will be able to have embryos screened for almost any defective gene, so that they have only healthy babies. In all this we are breaking new ethical ground. As one newspaper headline put it: 'Scientists playing God? We should rejoice.'

People spend vast sums of money today trying to slow down or hide the effects of the ageing process, but as someone pointed out, 'as soon as my pimples cleared up my hair started to fall out'. Another said: 'I have only this to say about growing old – I didn't notice it happening and I don't agree with it'; hence the rapid growth in cosmetic surgery.

The National Health Service is increasingly overstretched, not least financially. I like the card I bought for a patient in hospital which said: 'Over 17,500 people want you to get well very soon. They're in the queue for your bed.' The cost of new drugs is so great that some of the latest expensive life-savers are not widely available on the NHS because of the funding implications. The new financial reality has theological overtones – 'How much is a life worth?'

This brief survey of an ever-changing health scene will soon need revising, as new life-saving medical inventions arise from further breakthroughs in scientific research.

## Christianity and healing

Health is usually associated with the efficient functioning of the body, and healing with curing sickness and disease.

Christian healing, however, is not just about recovery from physical illness. A biblical understanding of health involves a close relationship between healing, wholeness and salvation. The New Testament word for salvation (soteria) conveys the idea of soundness of health in body, mind and spirit. So much unhappiness and ill-health is connected with our own mental well-being and the state of our relationships with each other, our environment and with God. Health is, therefore, a state of complete physical, mental, social and spiritual well-being. Christian sacraments of healing help foster this wholeness, although there will always be an incompleteness about healing that hints at a greater fulfilment to come.

Attention is increasingly being drawn in medical circles to the effects of religion on health. Various scientific projects, particularly in the USA, have shown the positive effects of spiritual activities on health and physical well-being that affect both quality of life and longevity. The increased interest being shown by the medical profession in spirituality and healing can be seen from this comment which appeared in an article in the *British Medical Journal* in December 2002:

> The World Health Organisation reports: 'until recently the health professionals have largely followed a medical model, which seeks to treat patients by focussing on medicine and surgery, and gives less importance to beliefs and faith in healing. This is no longer satisfactory. Patients and physicians have begun to realise the value of elements such as faith, hope and compassion in the healing process.' In one study 93% of patients with cancer said that religion helped sustain their hopes. Such high figures deserve our attention.

While in most European countries there has been a substantial dropping off of people who attend church services, there are increasing numbers who are seeking out Christian resources to alleviate their sickness and suffering, and many churches today offer healing services, prayer ministry, pastoral care and counselling, spiritual direction and other such support. Throughout history the Church has always cared for the sick and anxious in many different ways, whether through the establishment of Christian hospitals or by providing various pathways to wholeness such as those mentioned above.

There is also a bewildering variety of spiritual healers of various kinds outside the Church, many of dubious pedigree, as well as healing evangelists within who attract large crowds to their healing 'roadshows'. These charismatic preachers make extravagant claims concerning miracles of healing, as they expound the healing stories of Jesus in the Bible and expect them to be replicated through their own ministry.

In my book *Speaking of Healing* I wrote with preachers in mind as I examined how we can use the healing stories in the gospels to preach honestly and faithfully about healing today. In so doing I touched on many issues such as the relationship between Jesus' healing ministry and contemporary healing, the problem of evil and suffering, healing and the demonic, sickness as a punishment for sin and the link between faith and healing. I refer those wishing to look further at these controversial issues to that book.

Since writing *Speaking of Healing*, however, I have been conscious of comments made by a Roman Catholic priest, Jim McManus, who wrote in his book *The Healing Power of the Sacraments*: 'Talking about healing is one thing, praying to God for healing is quite another thing. If we remain simply on the level of talking, healing becomes just another speculative subject, something to discuss, something that may be of interest to a few people but which will never grip large numbers.'[1]

This book is aimed, therefore, not only at people like the clergy who have a professional interest in discussing such matters, but also at gripping the large number of people who are searching for healing and wholeness in their lives. The Church has a vital role to play in providing a healing, supportive,

caring community for such people and within this environment it makes available certain sacraments through which the
healing grace of God is dispensed. This book is about those
sacramental channels of grace and is written both to encourage the wounded to seek these sacraments of healing and also
to encourage the clergy to make them widely available as a
priority in their ministries.

## Sacraments

What is a sacrament? The word 'sacrament', let alone a definition of it, does not occur in scripture and the Church has
struggled with different definitions at different times. Professor
John Macquarrie, in his book *A Guide to the Sacraments*, comments that 'the Christian sacraments are so varied among
themselves that it is virtually impossible to give a definition of
"sacrament" that covers all cases'.[2] Without going into lengthy
technical and historical detail about what comprises a sacrament, the word derives from the Latin 'sacramentum', meaning a sacred sign or symbol. So a very succinct description
of Christian sacraments might be that they are sacred signs
instituted by Christ, through which God bestows his grace or
supernatural assistance upon us. The Church of England catechism in the Book of Common Prayer describes a sacrament
as 'an outward and visible sign of an inward and spiritual
grace'. These sacramental signs have been established by God,
who promises to mediate his presence to us through them.

In the Roman Catholic and Orthodox Churches there are
seven sacraments of the Church, namely: baptism, confirmation, the eucharist, penance (reconciliation), the anointing of
the sick, holy orders and matrimony. These seven sacraments
touch all the stages and important moments of Christian life.
Francis MacNutt, in his book *Healing*, comments:

> Since the sacraments are particularly chosen channels
> of God's saving power it is little wonder that they are

channels of healing, which is Christ's power to save applied to every area of human life. Three sacraments, Anointing of the Sick, Penance, and the Eucharist are specifically directed toward healing, while a fourth, Holy Orders, empowers the priest to heal the sick. In addition, I have seen healing connected with Baptism and with prayer for the renewal of Marriage. So I have seen healing in its connection with six of the sacraments; nor would I be surprised if healing, at least in its broader aspect of healing the whole man, were connected with Confirmation.[3]

Since the Reformation most Protestant Churches have retained only baptism and the eucharist as sacraments, which will require some comment later. 'Restricting the term "sacrament" to the two rites instituted by Christ is understandable from an historical perspective. However, in theological terms, it is somewhat arbitrary.'[4] In recent times 'the Ecumenical movement has caused theologians to look beyond the former Catholic–Protestant disputes about the number and nature of the sacraments to converge in a common understanding of Jesus as the supreme sacrament'.[5] So that when we receive the bread of life in the sacrament of the eucharist it is as though we are present with Christ in the upper room at his last supper on earth. When we are anointed with the 'oil of gladness'[6] in the sacrament of the anointing of the sick, it is as though Christ himself is stretching out his hand to heal us. When we receive forgiveness in the sacrament of reconciliation it is as though Christ is present in our midst speaking the words of forgiveness to us.

A sacramental sign is an efficacious sign. It actually makes present the thing it signifies. Stephen Cottrell, in his booklet *Sacraments, Wholeness and Evangelism*, comments:

Through the activity of the Holy Spirit sacraments continue the ministry of Jesus. He is still drawing people to the Father in baptism as he did throughout his ministry:

feeding his people in the Eucharist as he fed the 5000; healing his people in the sacrament of anointing as he healed
blind Bartimaeus; forgiving his people in the sacrament
of reconciliation as he forgave the woman caught in
adultery.[7]

This book is concerned with the sacraments of healing. I was
once asked to give a talk on 'the sacrament of healing'. That
is what the sacrament of the anointing of the sick with the
laying on of hands is sometimes referred to as. The Church of
England report *A Time to Heal* points out, however, that as
well as 'anointing and the laying on of hands, the ministry of
reconciliation (as confession in the presence of a priest is now
called) and Holy Communion are the means through which
the sick may encounter Christ the sacrament and hope for his
mercy and healing'.[8] We shall be looking in turn, therefore, at
these three sacraments of healing – the anointing of the sick,
penance (reconciliation) and the eucharist.

Much attention is often drawn in the healing ministry to
the role played by the preacher or so-called healer or healing
evangelist, which can sometimes be unhealthy. There is a
bewildering variety of healers, around some of whom personality cults have developed. How do we know whether God is
in this? With some it is doubtful whether he is, although there
are certainly those who do possess gifts of healing. Sacraments,
however, point away from the personality of the preacher/
healer. They are objective signs of God's presence. 'The sacraments provide an objective encounter with the risen Jesus, a
sure channel of grace through which the Spirit is poured. They
do not depend upon the eloquence or ability of the minister
but only on God's faithfulness.'[9]

Through these sacraments Jesus is made present to his
people. Many have yet to appreciate how much of God's healing power can flow through the sacraments of the anointing
of the sick, penance and the eucharist. I hope this book will

encourage us to make use of these healing channels or conduits of God's grace.

I generally receive about 250 Christmas cards each year, some of them quite splendid; but one year the most basic was the most precious, from a struggling single parent on a limited income. It was very imaginative and artistic: a piece of an old cardboard box with a sticky label still attached to it marked 'Fragile' and with a bit of string tied around it. It was a reflection of the fragility of that person's life and that of many others, and sometimes God has to come and put a bit of string around us to support us and hold us together. Macquarrie comments that the sacraments 'provide an ordered structure and support for the life of the Christian, from its beginning to its end',[10] and it is to those sacraments which bring healing that we now turn.

# 2

# *The sacrament of the anointing of the sick*

In this chapter we look at the laying on of hands with prayer and anointing of the sick. We examine the history, theology and liturgy of the sacrament and conclude with some interesting pastoral experiences. One amusing pastoral situation was that of a newly ordained priest apprehensively visiting a hospital ward. At one bed he asked a patient very nervously, 'Would you like me to pray with you?' – to which the patient replied, 'Well, if you think it will help you!' I hope that this study in prayer for healing of the sick will be of help to both priest and patient alike.

## Biblical background

Anointing is an ancient and biblical practice of blessing and empowerment. The kings of Israel were anointed and so the act became a sign of an outpouring of the Spirit of the Lord in divine blessing. The medicinal use of oil was widely accepted throughout the ancient Near East and this is reflected in both the Old and New Testaments. For example, oil is mentioned in the story of the Good Samaritan, who poured oil on the wounds of the injured traveller (Luke 10.34). The 'laying on of hands' which accompanies the anointing of the sick with oil is specifically used in Acts 9.17–19 by Ananias when healing St Paul of his blindness, after his conversion on the Damascus road. It is also used by Paul in healing Publius' father from fever in

Acts 28.7–10. It is further mentioned in Jesus' final commission to his disciples in the longer ending of Mark 16.18 where he says, 'they will lay their hands on the sick, and they will recover'.

With regard to anointing, Jesus is the Messiah, which is translated 'the anointed one' (John 1.41). There is, however, no explicit reference to Jesus, the anointed one, anointing with oil, for he *was* in a sense the oil. Nor was anointing specifically part of Christ's command to his disciples in Mark 6.7–13: 'He called the twelve and began to send them out two by two, and gave them authority over the unclean spirits . . . They cast out many demons, and anointed with oil many who were sick and cured them.' It's clear, I think, from this passage that although Christ did not explicitly command his disciples to anoint the sick, they nevertheless *did* anoint in his name and it must have carried his authority because many were healed.

In the letter of James there is also a clear injunction to pray over a sick person and anoint with oil:

Are any among you sick? They should call for the elders of the church and have them pray over them, anointing them with oil in the name of the Lord. The prayer of faith will save the sick, and the Lord will raise them up; and anyone who has committed sins will be forgiven. Therefore confess your sins to one another, and pray for one another, so that you may be healed. (James 5.14–16)

Even if Jesus' command is not explicit, both the laying on of hands and anointing have strong biblical precedent, although we do not have any real instructions regarding its practice except in James 5.

Some see James 5 as a bit of a problem: its expectation of immediate physical healing following prayer and anointing promises too much. I will return to this issue later. Note also how James 5 connects healing from sickness with confession of sins. Forgiveness of sins should be sought as God's way-in to seeking healing. The receiving of forgiveness and the act of forgiving others may open the way to healing and wholeness. In the story of the healing of the paralytic in Mark 2.1–12, healing and forgiveness seem to be linked. Jesus forgave the man his sins before telling him to get up and walk. I'm *not* saying, of course, that sickness is invariably caused by sin. We shall look at this connection more when we come to the sacrament of penance.

## Church history

From ancient times there is evidence of the anointing of the sick or unction in the Church's liturgical tradition, both in the east and in the west. The writings of Clement of Alexandria, Eusebius of Caesarea, and Irenaeus all refer to it, with the expectation of healing as a result. By the third century there appears to be a variety of practices, ranging from blessing and signing the affected part with the cross, to full laying on of hands with anointing. The Apostolic Tradition of Hippolytus (*c.* 215), which is the earliest known Christian prayer book, believed to have originated from Rome, contains a prayer of blessing over the oil for the sick. In the early fifth century a letter from Pope Innocent I indicates that the oil must be blessed by a bishop. As well as being used by the clergy in church services, it was also taken home by the lay people who used it whenever anyone in the home was sick. It seems there was a good deal of 'do-it-yourself' anointing in the early Church.

Up until the beginning of the ninth century anointing was used for the sick, with the ministry not restricted to the clergy, but there was no evidence of an actual Church ritual for anointing the sick. During the ninth century bishops in Charlemagne's Holy Roman Empire introduced a rite of anointing to be performed by priests alone and they forbade anointing of the sick by lay people. By the late Middle Ages, however, the liturgical history of the Church reflected a loss of the early Church's confidence in healing and there was, therefore, a gradual withdrawal from formal ministry to the sick. The Church, instead, became embroiled in more worldly affairs. Indeed, as early as the fourth century, Cyprian, the Bishop of Carthage in North Africa, was complaining that the healing ministry lacked strength in prayer because the Church was growing more worldly.

In the thirteenth century we have the story of Thomas Aquinas who, when he first visited Rome, was shown round the Vatican by the Pope to see all its wealth and treasures. The Pope (quoting from Acts 3 about the story of Peter healing the lame man begging at the beautiful gate) is reported to have said: 'No longer can the Church say with Peter of old, silver and gold have I none.' Thomas replied, picking up the biblical quotation, 'And neither can it say, "but what I do have I give to you: in the name of Jesus Christ of Nazareth rise up and walk".' Healing had become the exceptional miracle associated with sainthood, rather than the common practice of the Church. It was to the shrines of saints and martyrs, thought to be places of God's presence and power, that people would go in order to secure miracles, healing and other blessings.

MacNutt's book *The Nearly Perfect Crime* has the intriguing subtitle *How the Church Almost Killed the Ministry of Healing*. In it he explores how something so central to the gospel as healing almost died out.

By the twelfth century the focus of the sacrament of the anointing of the sick had shifted from healing to forgiveness of sins. The rite's prayers were adapted, so that instead of asking for healing they asked for forgiveness and salvation, which then confused the rite with the sacrament of penance. Likewise, oil was not placed on the parts of the body that were suffering but on the eyes, ears, mouth, hands and feet, through which the dying person might have sinned. The time for receiving the sacrament of anointing was also delayed to the deathbed when forgiveness of sins would be the final preparation for heaven. Because of this it received the name 'extreme unction', becoming associated with preparation for death rather than healing. Thus when the priest was called to the sick person, his presence wasn't an encouraging sign of hope, healing and recovery; it was more a dreaded sign that the end was near.

This association of the sacrament with death still lingers today. MacNutt tells the story of being asked not to visit a sick man in hospital in case the man might be frightened by the appearance of a priest and be worried before surgery that his condition was worse than it actually was. Rather than signifying healing, the priest's visit signalled the approach of death.[1]

By the Middle Ages, therefore, the anointing of the sick was practised as extreme unction and was conflated with the rite of penance and final communion (viaticum). The Church offered those who were about to leave this life the so-called 'last rites', the continuous rites of penance, the anointing of the sick and communion as viaticum (food for the journey, for the passing over). The reception of these sacraments at the completion of their earthly pilgrimage prepared them for their heavenly homeland.

The Council of Trent in 1551 stated that 'the Catholic Church professes and teaches that the anointing of the sick is one of the 7 sacraments of the New Testament, that it was instituted by Christ our Lord, is alluded to by Mark (6.13) and recommended to the faithful and promulgated by James the Apostle and brother of the Lord (James 5.14–15)'. As we have seen, sacraments are particular chosen channels of God's saving power and grace, through which the Spirit is poured and Jesus is made present to his people. Many Protestants, however, do not regard anointing of the sick as a sacrament, seeing it, at most, as a 'quasi-sacramental' action because of a lack of an explicit dominical command from the Lord to anoint the sick. They restrict the generic term 'sacrament' to baptism and holy communion only, as instituted by Christ himself.

At the time of the Reformation the reformers accepted only these two sacraments and denied the sacramental value of laying on of hands and anointing. They did not accept the evidence of Mark 6 as a basis for a rite of healing. For example, Martin Bucer condemned the superstition surrounding it and called for its abolition. He saw communion as being sufficient provision, for it was this 'by which the sick may be abundantly strengthened in health'.

While it is true that there is no explicit command of the Lord to anoint the sick as there is with baptism ('Go and baptize them in the name of . . .' Matthew 28.19) and communion ('Do this in remembrance of me . . .' Luke 22.19), we do have in Mark 6.13, as we have seen, an apostolic example of such practice and the passage in James 5 reinforces it. Catholics point out that the institution of this sacrament is supported by the text in Mark 6, which says that the disciples sent by Jesus anointed the sick, and that it is doubtful whether James would have recommended such a practice if it had not been ordained by Christ.

By the time of the Reformation healing had become downplayed. As MacNutt points out, Calvin 'strongly affirmed his belief in the remarkable healings worked by Jesus and his apostles when they laid their hands upon the sick. But Calvin also claimed that the healing ministry ceased after they had died; and, for him, the only thing left after the first century was superstition.'[2]

After the Reformation, because of the memory of the superstition, misuse and abuse of the sacrament of anointing, the Church of England was reluctant to use it. Its 1549 prayer book provided for anointing of the sick, but this did not find its way into the 1552 and 1662 prayer books. In the 1662 Book of Common Prayer, 'The Order for The Visitation of the Sick and The Communion of the Sick' functions 'on the presupposition that the person visited is under contract to die shortly; and almost says that he or she deserves it'.[3] In the west, therefore, unction remained a rite in the Roman Church, but for the dying only. A sacramental sign for healing had become a sacramental sign for dying.

15

In the centuries following the Reformation, there is evidence of a few healers at work, mainly in independent and Baptist churches. However, by the eighteenth century some theologians began denying that supernatural healing had ever taken place, even in Jesus' ministry, and this Enlightenment thinking continued into the twentieth century. By the beginning of the last century healing prayer had largely disappeared from the mainline historic churches and without it the healing ministry itself had become 'sickly'. All this was to change with the emergence of the pentecostal movement at the beginning of the twentieth century, followed by the charismatic renewal in all the major Christian denominations in the second half of the last century. This was followed by a 'third wave' towards the latter part of the century, which has led to the formation of numerous independent neo-charismatic churches throughout the world which practise the laying on of hands with prayer for healing, which may also be accompanied by the anointing of the sick, though without it being formally designated a sacrament. Meanwhile, as we shall see, changes were afoot in the Church of England and the Roman Catholic Church with regard to rites of anointing.

## Modern liturgies

It was not until the 1930s that the Church of England officially approved services for anointing and the laying on of hands. The Anglo-Catholic revival had helped lead to a recovery of the sacramental ministry towards healing. In 1983, following the introduction of the Alternative Service Book in the Church of England, a supplementary set of services was authorized under the title *Ministry to the Sick*, which provided a comprehensive liturgy for use with the sick including anointing and the laying on of hands.

This set of services was superseded by the new Church of England *Common Worship: Pastoral Services*, first published in

2000. These provide four forms of service for wholeness and healing that include the laying on of hands with prayer and anointing. One is for use with the sick at home or in hospital, the other three are for use in church services.

The first of these three services is 'A Celebration of Wholeness and Healing' especially suitable for a diocesan or deanery occasion. The laying on of hands and anointing (which is optional) take place after the liturgy of the word (i.e. the readings and sermon), and the prayers of intercession and penitence. If the liturgy of the eucharist then follows, the service continues with the Peace. Otherwise the service concludes with the Lord's Prayer, the Proclamation of the Gospel, the Peace and Dismissal.

The second form is for 'Laying on of Hands with Prayer and Anointing at a Celebration of Holy Communion' and is intended for occasional use, when appropriate, as part of the regular liturgical life of a parish. The structure is similar to the first form, except that the prayers of penitence are in the usual eucharistic setting at the beginning of the service. Where the laying on of hands and anointing is offered as part of regular Sunday worship, it may be done during the giving of communion.

The third form is 'Prayer for Individuals in Public Worship' and is primarily intended for use in churches where such prayer for individuals is a regular feature of Sunday worship. This public ministry of prayer may be accompanied by laying on of hands, and may also be accompanied by anointing with oil. In the context of a celebration of holy communion this personal ministry may be offered as part of the prayers of intercession, at the time of the giving of communion, or at the end of the service.

The theological introduction to these services of wholeness and healing states: 'Healing, reconciliation and restoration are integral to the good news of Jesus Christ. For this reason prayer for individuals, focussed through laying on of hands or anointing with oil, has a proper place within the public prayer of the Church.'[4]

In the Roman Catholic Church we have seen how the sacrament of the sick had in practice become the last anointing, the unction *in extremis* for those at the point of death. The Second Vatican Council (1962–65), however, wanted to remedy this situation and restore the original meaning of the sacrament. It therefore revised the sacrament of the anointing of the sick to widen its availability. Anointing 'is not a sacrament for those only who are at the point of death', but is intended for all who are seriously ill. Consequently, what was formerly called extreme unction 'may also and more fittingly be called "Anointing of the Sick"'.[5]

Three rites are provided for in the *Pastoral Care of the Sick: Rites of Anointing and Viaticum*; these are 'Anointing within Mass', 'Anointing outside Mass', and 'Anointing in a Hospital or Institution'. In the rite of anointing within mass the liturgy of anointing takes place between the liturgy of the word and the liturgy of the eucharist, that is, it follows the homily, and the mass resumes with the prayer over the gifts and the eucharistic prayer. The rites of anointing, both within and outside mass, may be used to anoint a number of people within the same celebration and are appropriate for large gatherings of a diocese, parish, or society for the sick, or for pilgrimages. However, the *Pastoral Care of the Sick* points out that the practice of indiscriminately anointing numbers of people on these occasions simply because they are ill or have reached an advanced age is to be avoided. The general introduction to these services states:

> This sacrament gives the grace of the Holy Spirit to those who are sick: by this grace the whole person is helped and saved, sustained by trust in God, and strengthened against the temptations of the Evil One and against anxiety over death. Thus the sick person is able not only to bear suffering bravely, but also to fight against it. A return to physical health may follow the reception of this

sacrament if it will be beneficial to the sick person's salvation.[6]

The sacrament of anointing for healing also has a high profile in the Orthodox Church. Whenever members of the congregation are sick, they are anointed. A particular service for healing is often held in Holy Week when the whole congregation is invited to be anointed, so that everyone has the opportunity to be anointed for healing at least once a year. In the Romanian Orthodox Church the sick are often anointed at the end of the celebration of the divine liturgy each Sunday.

I have briefly outlined above the liturgy of anointing in the Roman Catholic Church and the Church of England. The reader should consult the liturgical texts in each rite for further detail. We now go on to look at the administration of these rites.

## Administration of the sacrament

The introduction to the Roman Catholic rite of anointing of the sick states: 'The laying on of hands is clearly a sign of blessing, as we pray that by the power of God's healing grace the sick person may be restored to health or at least strengthened in time of illness . . . The practice of anointing the sick with oil signifies healing, strengthening, and the presence of the Spirit.'[7] There are three distinct and integral aspects to the celebration of this sacrament, namely the prayer of faith, the laying on of hands and the anointing with oil (also the blessing of the oil if it has not previously been blessed).

### The prayer of faith

Note that in the James 5 passage that refers to the anointing of the sick, it is the prayer of faith that will save the sick person. The prayer of faith to believe that healing can happen is an important ingredient in the effectiveness of this sacrament in conveying grace to the recipient. The absence of faith and repentance in a person may put an impediment in the way of the healing grace that would normally flow through this sacrament.

In Mark 11 Jesus said, 'Have faith in God' and in 11.24 goes on to say, 'I tell you, whatever you ask for in prayer, believe that you have received it, and it will be yours.' Christopher Hamel Cooke, one of my predecessors, who founded the St Marylebone Healing and Counselling Centre, wrote this:

> When we first proposed to hold healing services at St Marylebone Parish Church, one devout member of the congregation expressed her unease at the idea by asking if there was not a real danger that people might come expecting miracles. It would be a sad reflection on the state of the health of the Church if it abandoned its expectation of miracles or came to regard that expectation as dangerous.[8]

I suppose the ninth beatitude should be, 'Blessed are those who expect nothing for they shall not be disappointed.' On the other hand, those who claim to have no doubts are sometimes probably more in need of healing than those they pray for.

Because anointing is linked not only with faith but also with confession of sin in James 5, anointing is normally preceded by an act of penitence. I often use this Guild of Health prayer in preparation for healing:

> O God our Father, who is the source of all life and health, all strength and peace: Teach us to know you truly; take from us all that hinders the work of your healing power, all our sins, all our anxieties and fears, all resentment and hardness of heart; and help us to learn to enter into stillness and peace with you, and to know that you are our healer and redeemer; through Jesus Christ our Lord. Amen.

## The laying on of hands

A colleague told me the story of a woman who was visiting her elderly mother, who lived alone and was sometimes a little confused. When the daughter arrived at her mother's house, she met the GP who was just leaving. When she went inside and greeted her mother, her mother said, 'The vicar's just been to see me, he's such a nice man.' 'No, Mummy,' said her daughter, 'that wasn't the vicar, that was the doctor.' 'Really,' replied her mother, 'I thought he was a bit intimate!'

To lay hands on someone is to identify with the one to whom our hearts go out. Touch can also transmit the grace and healing power of God. Some involved in this ministry occasionally feel a tingling sensation in their fingers. In the story of the woman who touched the fringe of Jesus' clothes, power went out from him to heal her (Luke 8.43–48). In the gospels we read how the sick tried to touch him, for power came forth from him to heal them all (Mark 3.10; 6.56; Luke 6.19). Through the laying on of hands in the ministry of healing, Christ continues to touch us in order to heal us.

In the Roman Catholic rite the priest lays his hands on the head of the sick person in silence. In the Church of England rite the words used are:

> In the name of God and trusting in his might alone, receive Christ's healing touch to make you whole. May Christ bring you wholeness of body, mind and spirit, deliver you from every evil, and give you his peace. Amen.

The laying on of hands is lightly on the head and/or shoulder, and in the Church of England can be administered by a lay person, not only by a priest. A person may also receive the laying on of hands on behalf of others who are not present, as well as for themselves.

## Anointing

The outward anointing of the body with oil signifies the inward anointing of the person with the Holy Spirit who is the agent of all healing. The sick person is anointed on the forehead and on the hands in the Roman rite, or on other parts of the body in the eastern rite. The Roman rite also authorizes the priest to anoint additional parts of the body, for example, the area of pain or injury. The norm in the Anglican rite is to anoint on the forehead with the sign of the cross, but provision is also made for anointing on the hands in some circumstances. In the Roman Catholic rite for the anointing of the sick, the words of administration used when making the sign of the cross in oil are:

> Through this holy anointing may the Lord in his love and mercy help you with the grace of the Holy Spirit. Amen [on the forehead]. May the Lord who frees you from sin save you and raise you up. Amen [on the palms of both hands].

In the Church of England rite the words are:

> N . . . I anoint you in the name of God who gives you life. Receive Christ's forgiveness, his healing and his love. May the Father of our Lord Jesus Christ grant you the riches of his grace, his wholeness and his peace. Amen.

In both Roman and Anglican rites the oil used is normally olive oil and is either blessed during the liturgy of anointing by the bishop or priest presiding, or has previously been consecrated by the bishop on Maundy Thursday at the Chrism Mass. In the Roman Catholic Church the priest alone administers both the laying on of hands and anointing. In the Church of England it is expected that the oil be administered by the presiding priest, but delegation to other authorized ministers is allowed. It is not clear whether this means a priest and only a priest can administer the anointing. Some believe that it would be consistent with the understanding of the administration of communion to allow a lay person to administer not only the eucharistic elements, but also to minister the oil to a sick person (whether at home or in the church), given that a lay person can administer the laying on of hands.

## Blessing of the oil

The Roman Catholic *Pastoral Care of the Sick: Rites of Anointing and Viaticum* states that 'the prayer for blessing the oil of the sick reminds us, furthermore, that the oil of anointing is the sacramental sign of the presence, power and grace of the Holy Spirit'.[9] In the Roman rite the blessing invokes divine favour upon *both* the oil and the recipients:

> God of all consolation, you chose and sent your Son to
>     heal the world.
> Graciously listen to our prayer of faith:
> send the power of your Holy Spirit, the Consoler, into this
>     precious oil, this soothing ointment, this rich gift, this
>     fruit of the earth.
> Bless this oil and sanctify it for our use.
> Make this oil a remedy for all who are anointed with it;
> heal them in body, in soul and in spirit,
> and deliver them from every affliction.
> We ask this through our Lord Jesus Christ, your Son,
> who lives and reigns with you and the Holy Spirit,
> one God, for ever and ever. Amen.

There are two forms of prayer over the oil in the Church of England *Common Worship* rite, but the emphasis in both is not on any supposed impact of the Spirit upon the oil itself, but on its use and benefits to the recipients. The oil is obviously not to be seen as magical in some way.

## Frequency of use

While the anointing of the sick is always accompanied by the laying on of hands, the latter can be administered alone. Many churches today, including non-liturgical churches, offer a regular ministry of laying on of hands and prayer for healing without anointing with oil. There is no definitive distinction drawn in scripture between the laying on of hands and anointing, though the use of oil would seem to give it a weightier understanding.

The traditional difference of emphasis between anointing and the laying on of hands has been that anointing is ministered less frequently, being reserved for more acute cases. Carolyn Headley writes in her booklet *The Laying on of Hands and Anointing*: 'Many involved in the healing ministry hold anointing to be of a different nature to the laying on of hands, as a profound act, requiring thorough preparation with counselling and serious reflection and confession prior to ministry. It is seen as applicable to those with deep illnesses, or people who are organically sick with their illnesses.'[10] It is not just for physical illness, however. It is concerned with wholeness and is therefore for the healing of body, mind and spirit, these being interconnected.

The laying on of hands can be administered by lay people in the Church of England, though they should have some training and recognition for any formal exercise of the ministry. There is no reason why individuals should not receive the laying on of hands frequently, so long as it does not become an addiction. A note in the 1983 Church of England *Ministry to the Sick* services suggests that the laying on of hands is to be seen as appropriate for more frequent and informal use than anointing. It states that anointing 'should be used more sparingly than the laying on of hands, and is especially appropriate for use when a sick person is at a time of crisis'.[11] This does not suggest, however, that it is unrepeatable for there may be many times of crisis, or near crisis.

Many priests follow the traditional custom of reserving anointing for these times of crisis, such as the diagnosis of a life-threatening disease or prior to an operation. The Church of England gives no official guidance on whether anointing can be administered often, leaving it to the discretion of the clergy. In the Roman Catholic Church the sacrament of anointing is used only for those whose health is seriously impaired by sickness or old age. The Catechism states that it is particularly fitting to receive this sacrament just prior to a serious operation. The sacrament may be repeated if the sick person recovers after being anointed and then again falls ill, or if during the same illness the person's condition becomes more serious.

## Objectivity of the sacrament

A bishop, when preaching at the Chrism Mass at St Paul's Cathedral one Maundy Thursday, commented to the congregation that he particularly liked the sacrament of the anointing of the sick because it didn't rely on the gifts of the minister. I think that is a very important point, particularly when you see some healing evangelists at work. I remember seeing a huge poster outside a railway station advertising 'Michael Reid Ministries'. It had on it in bold lettering 'Miracles – Healing – Faith' and then underneath a picture of a man (presumably Michael Reid) clutching a microphone with a child in his arms. There was no reference to God, the attention centred on the healer/evangelist.

A television documentary showed Benny Hinn preaching at an evangelistic meeting at Norwich City Football Stadium. As he invited people up on to the stage to be healed, orchestrating the crowd as he did so, he shouted out, 'If you don't get better it's not my fault!' This implied that if people were not healed it was not because of Benny Hinn (or the God he represented), but presumably either because of people's lack of faith or because of their sin. Here he was ordering people to get better. What damage was that doing to those struggling to live with disabilities that are beyond medical cure? Not only will they in all probability have to continue to live with their disability, but now it is also their fault if they remain disabled. Rather than increasing their faith in God, surely it would actually destroy it.

Nevertheless, there are those who do benefit from the ministries of these healing evangelists. As one such evangelist said to a clergyman who was criticizing how he was conducting his healing ministry: 'Well, at least I prefer my way of doing it to your way of not doing it!'

As I mentioned earlier, however, sacraments point away from the personality of the minister. They do not depend upon the eloquence or ability of the minister, but only upon God, because Christ is the true minister of every sacrament. They are objective signs of his presence rather than based upon the subjective moods, or worthiness or unworthiness of the minister or the one seeking healing.[12]

There is, of course, the danger and mistake of elevating the holy oil to the same pedestal as a preacher like Benny Hinn. I remember being called to the bedside of a young woman who was dying of breast cancer. The once beautiful face of this young woman was now unrecognizable, her hair long gone and her face terribly jaundiced. The bed was surrounded by her family and her father exclaimed, 'Here comes the vicar with the holy oil blessed by the bishop!' as though it was some magic potion.

In the remainder of this chapter I want to look at some pastoral situations in relation to this sacrament and the various effects that can follow prayer for healing: namely when healing does not occur, when it occurs but then there is a relapse, when healing happens gradually, or when it happens instantly.

## When James 5 fails

People of faith cannot avoid asking hard questions posed by suffering. When the Anglican bishop John Robinson was struck down with terminal cancer at the height of his powers he was reported to have said, 'It is easy to see God in the sunset, but it is very hard to see him in the cancer.' Certain words uttered in the face of tragedy stick in my memory. In one church I remember a heartbroken father, whose daughter had been knocked down by a car and killed as she crossed the road outside her own house, saying, 'I should be buying her a wedding dress not a coffin.' While heroic efforts were going on to save lives following the Indian Ocean tsunami disaster on Boxing Day 2004, which showed the generosity of the human spirit in responding to disaster, the *Daily Mail* carried the headline: 'Kindness – Amidst the horror, it's the only thing we can really have faith in'.

Or *The Times* headline on 5 January 2006: 'Miracle that never was leaves grieving families asking why'. The families of 12 miners trapped by an underground explosion in West Virginia, USA were told that their loved ones were alive. When they heard the news they exclaimed 'It's a miracle', and in the Baptist church where they had been waiting and praying they burst into singing the hymn 'How great thou art'. Three hours later they were told they had been misinformed and that all 12 were dead. When told the news one of their number said, 'We don't know that there is even a Lord any more. We thought it was a miracle and it was taken away from us.'

Some will ask, why doesn't God intervene today as he intervened (according to the scriptures) in the past? It is not easy to explain a God who fails to prevent some human tragedy, but who will respond, for instance, to a request for a miracle of healing. Similarly, when the Bible encourages Christians to pray for healing and leads them to expect recovery to result from such prayer (as indicated in James 5.14–16 or Mark 16.18), it becomes a battle of faith when these raised hopes and expectations are dashed to the ground when healing does not occur.

I once went to visit a woman, the wife of a priest colleague, who was dying of lung cancer. She had much to teach us all about faith and courage during her illness. I asked her if she would like me to anoint her. She was hesitant at first, to my surprise, given that I knew her trust in the promises of God and her knowledge of the James 5 text. She was concerned that if nothing should change and she did not recover, the faith of others might be damaged. How sensitive. I understood, for I have been there myself.

When I was training for the priesthood I had to produce a short paper on 'The use of the Bible'. I chose as my subject 'What is the point of petitionary prayer?' based on the James 5 text. I chose it because my wife had recently been prayed for by someone who came to the theological college who had the gift of healing. My wife had received the laying on of hands, but she was not healed. I felt that God had let her down, although all was to be well some time later.

I was very angry with God and let this come out in my short paper, which was much shorter than it should have been because I was so angry. This is what I simplistically wrote as a fresh ordinand back in 1970 (hence biblical quotations are from the Revised Standard Version and are not gender inclusive):

What is the point of petitionary prayer? I wish to answer this question with reference to one specific area of prayer – prayer for healing. I wish to do this by drawing on one text only from the Bible. I then want to ask how we can take this text in our use of the Bible. The text is James 5.14–16: 'Is any among you sick? Let him call for the elders of the church, and let them pray over him, anointing him with oil in the name of the Lord; and the prayer of faith *will* save the sick man, and the Lord *will* raise him up . . . pray for one another, that you may be healed.' The point of petitionary prayer in this case is that the prayer of faith *will* save the sick man and the Lord *will* raise him up, and if this does not happen then there is no point in the petitioner's prayer in this case, because the text is quite unwavering in its confident assertion that the Lord will heal.

How *do* we use this text in our bibles? Precisely in the way in which it tells us to use it, and we must expect the results that it claims. If we don't get them, then the text and the prayer are pointless and useless. Now ministers and theologians will come along and qualify the meaning of the text for you (even though the text will carry no qualification itself). And the minister will comfort you if the text fails by quoting other texts for you from the Bible which are supposed to alleviate your distress, such as 'all things work together for good for those who love God' etc. But the point is this, that if the text of James 5 is found to be meaningless, then so are the other qualifying texts that people glibly give you in your distress. If the James text is meaningless, then so are the qualifiers.

This is a 'use of the Bible' paper. This text (James 5.14–16) has got to be used and used in the way it asks to be used; and used in the confidence that the prayer will be answered in the way the text indicates. I submit that the text is meaningless if you qualify it – until as Professor Flew would say: 'it dies the death of a thousand qualifications'. I know that the text will be qualified by all and sundry, with such words used as 'mystery', 'we cannot understand the ways of God', 'blessing comes out of suffering', 'it was not his will' etc. But this makes the text meaningless and unusable. The text must be taken as it stands and used as it stands. If it fails in experience then it also becomes meaningless – and more than that, it becomes FALSE, and the point of petitionary prayer becomes that of a person trying to clutch at a straw which cannot hold him/her.

My tutor was later to become an archbishop. This is what he wrote at the bottom of my paper:

The trouble with this approach is that it is too limited. If you are going to work out a theology of petitionary prayer, you *cannot* base it completely on one text! On your argument Jesus' prayer in the Garden of Gethsemane was pointless and useless. God did not answer it! What about Job? What about Elijah – mentioned in James as an example of faith – whose ministry ends in failure! I believe God answers prayer – indeed, I *know* God answers prayer, but he is a sovereign God and acts according to his purpose in the world and Church. It may not be His will for someone to be cured in the way we expect. Look how Paul's prayer for healing was *never* answered in the way he expected! (2 Corinthians 12).

My tutor was drawing attention to Paul's thorn in the flesh. Paul appealed to the Lord three times for this thorn (whatever it was) to leave him but it was not removed. Instead the Lord said, 'My grace is sufficient for you, for my power is made perfect in weakness' (2 Corinthians 12.9). Needless to say, I got the bottom mark for my naivety. The application of scriptural texts depends so much on how we interpret the Bible.

## Healing followed by relapse

In the late 1970s, when I was vicar of an urban London parish, there was a lovely West Indian called Joe in the congregation who was very interested in the ministry of healing. A friend of his, Edna, was in the London Homoeopathic Hospital and he would go to visit her. Being an outgoing sort of person, while he was visiting his friend he would have a chat with other people on the ward.

The woman in the next bed to his friend was a nurse called Sheila who had come down from Norfolk to be treated for multiple sclerosis. She had been in a wheelchair for two years and was now trying homoeopathy as a last resort. She had been in the hospital for five weeks, during which time Joe had seen her several times and talked to her at length about God. He said that he would get his vicar to visit her to pray with her. Better still, he suggested that if the hospital would allow it he would arrange for her to be taken out of hospital one afternoon and brought to our church some six miles away, and we could pray for her there. I was not very pleased with Joe's evangelistic efforts, as I had enough sick people to look after without acting as a hospital back-up. The hospital was agreeable to this happening, presumably thinking there was nothing to lose.

So one afternoon Sheila was taken in a wheelchair from the hospital ward and driven back to our church, with the wheelchair bundled into the boot of the car. On arrival we wheeled Sheila across the vicarage grounds to the church. My elderly father was sitting on the veranda in front of the house and as we passed him I said, 'Hello, Dad, we're just taking this lady into the church to pray for her. She can't walk.'

In the church, Sheila was wheeled first to the font where she was baptized, and then into the side chapel where the blessed sacrament was kept. She received the laying on of hands and I anointed her and gave her holy communion from the reserved sacrament, as one desirous of being confirmed, and then we left her in her wheelchair for a few minutes to pray silently. When we returned she said that she felt strength returning to her legs, so we lifted her out of the wheelchair and with our assistance she began to take a few tentative steps around the church. As the strength returned to her legs she began to walk unaided, gradually gathering speed. It was a time of tears and great rejoicing.

Sheila said that she wanted to go and visit Joe's friend Edna, who had been in the next bed to her and had now been discharged from hospital. We left the church, therefore, and walked across the church grounds, passing the vicarage where my father was still sitting outside. Sheila was now walking unaided, with me pushing the empty wheelchair. As we walked past my father, I winked and he said in amazement, 'Bugger me!' We drove to Edna's house and I walked up the garden path and pressed the doorbell, leaving Sheila back at the garden gate. When Edna opened the front door I said, 'We've brought a friend to see you.' Sheila walked up the path to the door and the two women embraced each other, crying tears of joy.

We took Sheila back to the hospital. The next day, she told me, she did three miles on the exercise bike; following that she was discharged with a clean bill of health. The hospital's explanation for her symptoms miraculously disappearing was that she was either having a remission from the disease, or that she had been wrongly diagnosed and did not have MS in the first place. Sheila came back to the church a few months later to recount her story to the congregation.

However, about a couple of years after her discharge she wrote telling me that she was now having difficulty in walking again and had been rediagnosed as having MS. Her own explanation of what had happened was that she had had MS, that she had experienced a miraculous healing, and now she had MS again. She said that she had just been confirmed by the Bishop of Norwich in his private chapel; although slightly battered, she had emerged with a stronger conviction than ever in God's strength to help her overcome her difficulties.

I often wondered what happened to Sheila over the following years, for she moved and I lost touch with her. However, I managed to track her down again recently after 25 years or so, to find that she is living alone with her two dogs and suffering ongoing health problems. She said that her faith was as strong as ever and that it gave her comfort and kept her going.

## Gradual healing

In my experience, for nearly everyone who is anointed, if a cure is to take place it is a gradual process. One should not be surprised by this. After all, this is the way that modern medicine and the body works. A good example of gradual healing is told by Sister Briege McKenna in her book *Miracles Do Happen*:

Once when I was giving a retreat with Fr. Kevin Scanlon in Australia, I met a sister who had been crippled by polio. She had braces on her legs and a back brace. After Father Kevin administered the sacrament of anointing, she sat for eight hours in the chapel. During that entire period, she stayed in one position and her entire body was shaking. I felt sure that she was experiencing the beginning of a progressive healing. I went over to her and said, 'Sister, God is healing you.'

I read later in a magazine that daily for four months, as she rested, her whole body would begin shaking again. The doctor explained that her tissues and muscles that were withered because of the polio were being brought back to life. He told her she was in the process of being healed. The braces were removed.

The healing didn't happen the day she was anointed. It began that day and it continued. The last time I heard, it was still continuing. Her body, the doctor explained, was being reconstructed under the anointing of God.[13]

I received the following e-mail, quite out of the blue, from a young woman:

> Well hello there, it's been a very long time since I have seen or spoken to you. I bet you are wondering who this is. It's Emma Hickling here, who was seriously ill in 1986 and was diagnosed with having systemic lupus erythematosus. You came to my bedside when I was in the Brompton Hospital every night and spent some time with me on my own healing me. My mum from this day always says she is sure you have something to do with me surviving. I was only 9 then, now I am 25. The years have flown very quickly. I am very well now, I only have to go to the hospital once every 6 months for check-ups. I don't live in London anymore. My parents & I moved to Lincolnshire nearly 2 years ago. I work full time as a nursery nurse looking after children aged 2–3 years. I love it. How are you and your family? Give my regards to Mrs Gower. I often

talk about you both a lot. My parents send their regards
to you. Love Emma

I remember Emma well. My wife had taught her in our church
school. She had indeed been very sick. I wasn't sure what sys-
temic lupus erythematosus was, either then or now. When I got
the e-mail I asked the crown churchwarden at St Marylebone,
who is a retired consultant, about the condition, and how
to pronounce it! He informed me that Hugh Gaitskell, the
one-time leader of the Labour Party, had died from it and
that in those days it had been very difficult to treat. Anyway, I
recall travelling up to central London from my parish near
Heathrow airport on a number of evenings and administering
the laying on of hands and also anointing Emma with the oil
of healing. With skilled medical care and prayer for God's
grace through this sacrament, she lived to send me an e-mail
16 years later. Such conditions, however, require continual
monitoring.

## *Instant healing*

Sometimes when people receive the sacrament of the anointing of the sick things happen immediately. One such recent
incident stands out in my memory in my capacity as chaplain
to the London Clinic, one of six private hospitals I look after
in the Harley Street area of central London. I visited a titled
woman, a prominent church person, who had just had an
operation for cancer. We talked for about 45 minutes and it
was clear that she was struggling to come to terms with the
ramifications of her illness. Her surgeon had told her that the
operation had been successful, but her recovery would be slow
and she would require many months of chemotherapy followed
by radiotherapy. She said that she didn't know how she could
face all this. She just didn't want to have to go through it all.
We prayed that God would give her the strength to do so and

I gave her holy communion, the laying on of hands and anointing. I then left her to visit a patient in another hospital nearby.

When I got back to the office about an hour after leaving
this lady, her daughter telephoned to ask me at what time my
visit had ended. I said about an hour ago. She said, 'That's astonishing. She died ten minutes or so after you left.' This is not
much of an encouragement for those who ask me to anoint them,
but maybe God in his providence, knowing that this lady just
couldn't face the future ahead of her, released her from this
life to take her to himself.[14] I had anointed for healing, but it
turned out to be the last anointing for her immediate depar-
ture from this life. In her case it was to be her ultimate healing, which spared her more suffering.

This sacrament is not just about praying for physical healing, but also for other inner forms of healing. On one occasion I visited a retired colonel in the King Edward VII's Sister
Agnes Hospital, where I am also the chaplain, to give him holy
communion and to pray for his healing as requested. He had
just had a hip replacement, but of more concern to him was
that he was suffering from an emotional problem. Whenever
he entered into conversation with anyone he would begin to
cry after a while. Several weeks after administering the sacrament to him and asking God to heal him of his emotional
problem, he wrote to me from home: 'I want to tell you that
from that day until now I have not had a single emotional
episode. I am completely cured and my new hip is doing well
too. I do thank God and I thank you too as his instrument.
I am truly grateful. I will gladly pass on this story.'

God is also not tied to healing at the specific moment of
the anointing when administering the sacrament. I once con-
ducted a Sunday eucharist which included within it the laying
on of hands and anointing of the sick. At the end of the
service, when I thought everyone had gone, I disrobed and
was about to leave the church when I saw a young woman
sobbing in the pew. I went up to her thinking she was perhaps

upset because she had not been healed. She was clutching her ribcage and I assumed she was in pain. She told me that she was crying tears of joy because, if I remember her story correctly, a few years before she had fallen heavily on her hand and fractured her wrist. She had not received any medical treatment at the time until it was too late, and had now experienced a loss of feeling in that hand. This meant that occasionally this would cause problems; for example, she had burnt herself when using the oven without realizing it. But while she was at the service, actually during the reading of the gospel which was a healing story of Jesus, such was the power of the Lord present to heal that feeling returned to her hand. God did not wait for the laying on of hands and anointing. She was clutching her ribcage because she could hardly believe the restoration of feeling she was experiencing and her tears were tears of joy.

Another story comes from the July 2000 edition of *Alpha News*, which carried a full page article entitled 'God gave me back my sight'. It was the story of a woman called Jean Smith, from Newport, South Wales, who had been blind for over 16 years. At the end of an Alpha Course she was attending, a holy communion service with prayer for healing and anointing was held. During that service Jean received anointing with oil and was healed of her blindness. As she describes it:

> I was anointed with oil from Galilee which had been blessed. I was led back to my seat. As I continued in prayer, I wiped the perspiration from my forehead, and in so doing rubbed the oil into my eyes. When I opened them I could see the cross and communion on the altar table. Thinking it was my imagination I closed them again. Upon opening them a second time, the tears flowed as I now realised a miracle had occurred and I could see. There was not a dry eye in the church.

I have chosen this story to recount because at the time I was in correspondence with Dr Peter May, a Christian family doctor in Southampton, who questions many of the miraculous claims made by preachers involved in the healing ministry, which can get exaggerated in the telling. I asked him what he made of this story. He stated that he had been in correspondence with the Alpha organization on several occasions because he wanted to make contact with Jean Smith to try and obtain the case notes from her doctor, but he had been unable to elicit a reply. Maybe in this case all that needs to be said are the words of the man born blind in John 9 after Jesus had healed him. He said he didn't know how it happened, but 'One thing I do know, that though I was blind, now I see' (9.25). I am reminded of something said, in another connection, by a former editor of the *Sunday Times*: 'This story's too good to check.'

In this chapter we have looked at the history, theology and liturgy of this sacrament, and then at the various effects that can result from prayer for healing. These are not exhaustive: for example, people may not be completely healed but their condition is improved; or they are sustained and strengthened by God through this sacrament so they become better able to cope with their suffering.

In the Conclusion of this book I look at the distinction between curing and healing, which Macquarrie comments on in connection with this sacrament of the anointing of the sick (unction):

> In thinking about unction it is therefore important to distinguish between curing and healing. Curing has to do with relieving or removing the physical illness, whatever it may be . . . Unction does not guarantee cure. It may sometimes help toward a cure . . . But its aim is to heal the entire person. That could mean that although the physical condition is not cured, the sick person is enabled to integrate even his or her suffering into the personality and to become a better person in the process.[15]

# 3

# *The sacrament of penance and reconciliation*

———◆————

In this chapter we look at the sacrament of penance/ reconciliation, or the sacrament of confession as it has more commonly been known until recently. For most people it conjures up the image of the Roman Catholic priest in his confessional box hearing people's confessions, which is foreign territory for Anglican and Protestant Christians. However, in 2006 the Church of England brought out its own rites/services of reconciliation, which has given the practice of auricular confession a more prominent position in the life of the Anglican Church. It is, therefore, a most opportune time to discuss this sacrament. I will be examining its biblical basis, and its place in the history of the Church and in modern liturgical practice. I will also explore the human need that this sacrament is designed to meet and its place as a sacrament of healing.

This sacrament deals with the healing of our sins. A preacher once stated that there are 296 different sins; his mailbox was subsequently filled each day with requests for a list of them from people who were afraid that they'd been missing something. A letter appeared in the correspondence pages of a national newspaper on the subject of confessions, which said: 'Sir, I find, at a fairly advanced age, that to my regret I have nothing worth confessing. Yours truly . . .' Sin, however, is not something to be welcomed, given its destructive effect on human life. Since earliest times Christians have had sacraments and rituals of repentance and reconciliation to deal with sin, and we shall first explore the historical background to these.

## Biblical background

The Bible treats sin with the utmost seriousness, for it is ultimately seen as rebellion against God which separates us from him, provokes his judgement and wrath and brings suffering and sorrow upon ourselves and those around us. The Old Testament prophets denounced the sins of the Hebrew people, calling them to repent, while assuring them that they were still loved by God, who will never abandon them, no matter how great their sins may be.

The gospels record that the call to repentance, heralded by John the Baptist, was a central part of Jesus' teaching and that during his ministry he both forgave sins and exhorted his followers to forgive one another. They also portray Jesus' compassion towards those who were publicly identified as sinners. To his self-righteous detractors he said: 'Those who are well have no need of a physician, but those who are sick; I have come to call not the righteous but sinners' (Mark 2.17). Indeed, 'Jesus came into the world to save sinners' (1 Timothy 1.15) through his sin-bearing death on the cross. Among his last words was the word of forgiveness spoken and demonstrated from the cross, 'Father, forgive them' (Luke 23.34).

It has been said that if you want to know what God thinks of sin look at the cross, for the message of the gospel is centred upon it. It is a message about forgiveness that we do not deserve and we cannot earn. There is no sin, however great, that is greater than the love of God demonstrated on the cross of Calvary. Any discussion about confession is rooted here. This forgiveness is also expressed in drinking from the cup of wine in remembrance of Jesus' death in the sacrament of holy communion: 'This is my blood of the covenant, which is poured out for many for the forgiveness of sins' (Matthew 26.28).

The call to repent was continued by his apostles. On the day of Pentecost Peter exhorted the crowd to 'repent, and be baptized every one of you in the name of Jesus Christ so that your sins may be forgiven' (Acts 2.38). The Christian ceremony and sacrament that spoke explicitly of the forgiveness of sins was that of baptism, later formulated in the Nicene Creed with the words 'we acknowledge one baptism for the forgiveness of sins'. To be baptized is to identify with Christ's death and resurrection: 'Do you not know that all of us who have been baptized into Christ Jesus were baptized into his death? Therefore we have been buried with him by baptism into death, so that, just as Christ was raised from the dead by the glory of the Father, so we too might walk in newness of life' (Romans 6.3–4).

There is strong biblical support for believing that Jesus' authority to absolve people from their sins (Mark 2.10) has been passed to the Church, which acts as God's agent in mediating his forgiving grace. In John's gospel we read that Jesus said to his disciples: 'Receive the Holy Spirit. If you forgive the sins of any, they are forgiven them; if you retain the sins of any, they are retained' (John 20.22–23). This text is contained in the ordination service for priests. Jesus seems to anticipate the authority of the Church in this respect when he says: 'I tell you, you are Peter, and on this rock I will build my church, and the gates of Hades will not prevail against it. I will give you the keys of the kingdom of heaven, and whatever you bind on earth will be bound in heaven, and whatever you loose on earth will be loosed in heaven' (Matthew 16.18–19).

It would appear from these texts that Jesus placed absolution and the authority to release people from their sins in the mouth of the Church. We do not know, however, how the early Church exercised this authority of binding or loosing, forbidding and allowing, though Paul seems to recommend such a practice in the Corinthian Church (see 1 Corinthians 5 and 2 Corinthians 2). Another example of this binding and loosing can be found in Matthew 18.15–18.

In the gospels there are two occasions recorded where Jesus appears to heal by first proclaiming the forgiveness of sins – the healing of the paralytic in Mark 2 and the man at the pool of Bethzatha in John 5. A further reference in the New Testament to confession of sin can be found in James 5.16 alongside the practice of the anointing of the sick, which links it with healing: 'Therefore confess your sins to one another, and pray for one another, so that you may be healed.' Morton comments:

> Some form of mutual confession is suggested in James 5.13–20 and it appears the local church elders had a role to play in ministering God's forgiveness through prayer. This evidence is too flimsy to suggest that Confession existed in the modern sense, but the New Testament certainly provides two important foundations for later development; the authority of the Church to minister absolution and the appropriateness of Christians confessing to one another, at least in certain circumstances.[1]

## Church history

In baptism sins are forgiven and that should, therefore, be the end of sin. However, sin is so deeply rooted in human existence that it cannot easily be got rid of. As baptism is given only once, it soon became apparent that some supplementary sacrament was required, which eventually became the sacrament of penance.

Beyond the New Testament, there existed during the first Christian centuries a rigorous penitential system for dealing with baptized Christians who had fallen into serious or mortal sin. The Church in New Testament times had already begun to distinguish between grave sins and venial sins that are less serious,

as can be seen from 1 John 5.16–17: 'There is sin that is mortal
. . . All wrongdoing is sin, but there is sin that is not mortal.'

Church leaders faced a particular problem of how to re-admit into the Church those who in the face of persecution had renounced their faith and offered sacrifices to Roman gods. In some places Christians who had committed grave sins were put through the process of baptism a second time, but this was clearly not satisfactory, for baptism is a once-and-for-all event (Ephesians 4.5). A rigorous penitential discipline was therefore established for those who had committed particularly grave sins after baptism, such as apostasy, idolatry, murder and adultery. This penitential system allowed for the reconciliation and readmission of repentant sinners, although this absolution was available only once in a person's lifetime. It could not be repeated lest people think they could commit serious sins and be forgiven as often as they liked.

Those who had scandalized the Church by committing major sins would be admitted, either voluntarily or under threat of excommunication, to the Order of Penitents by the bishop. The penitent would undertake a strict regime of spiritual discipline including prayer, fasting, almsgiving and other works of public penance that would show their willingness to repent of their sin. This penance might even include the wearing of sackcloth and ashes; and at the eucharist the penitent would stand apart from the rest of the community and was not allowed to share com-munion. The period of repentance might last for a few months or even several years, according to the gravity of the sin. When the bishop was satisfied that the penitent had been re-converted they were admitted back into the eucharistic fellowship.

The severity of this system worked well when Christians were few in number, but when the Roman Emperor Constantine espoused Christianity and converts poured into the Church the system began to fail, its severity eventually leading to its break-down. The more Christians there were the more backsliders, the more sins that required public penance and the more severe and lengthy the penances. Converts, therefore, increasingly postponed becoming public penitents until later in life when penances would be shorter, often putting off their baptism until the eve of their death when they would then receive absolution from the bishop.

The penitential system fell into disuse following the fall of the Roman Empire and was eventually replaced. A new system began to emerge through the influence of Celtic and Anglo-Saxon monasticism, which was in turn inspired by the eastern monastic tradition. Private and repeated confession of faults to a confessor was a common practice in monasteries. From the seventh century onwards, Irish monks and others were sent as missionaries to continental Europe, and they brought with them this private practice of penance, which offered various advantages over the old system. Public and prolonged completion of penitential works before reconciliation with the Church was no longer required. The new practice was performed in secret between penitent and priest and rather than penance being undergone once in a lifetime it could now be repeated as often as was needed. This practice was extended to the faithful, opening up the way for regular private confession as part of normal church life.

In 1215 the practice received official support when the Fourth Lateran Council declared that all communicants were obliged to go to confession at least once a year. This development meant that the authority to minister absolution was extended from the bishop to all priests, and manuals gave guidance on the setting of penances to ensure uniformity. It was from these roots that modern confessional practice grew.

In this study on sacraments of healing it should be noted that the new system, rather than emphasizing penitential discipline, was concerned more with spiritual health, and medical metaphors were not uncommon. Sin, for example, was seen as an ulcerating wound that required to be laid bare before the physician (the priest) that it might be healed.[2] Historically, a medicinal understanding of the sacrament of penance had particularly been stressed in the eastern Church, penance being seen as a medicine for healing past sins and preserving from future sins.

During the Middle Ages the milder penances now assigned by priests were felt by some scholastic theologians to be insufficient to satisfy God's justice and so they developed the theory of purgatory, that at death most souls would have to undergo a painful period of purgation before being allowed to enter heaven. To the medieval mind satisfaction had to be made for sins, like a debt to be paid. Merit could be earned, however, which would remit sin and its punishment. Indulgences were granted, therefore, for doing good works, giving alms to the poor, donating to the Church, performing various religious rituals and the like. The merit accumulated was applied not only to the living but also to the dead, leading to the belief that one could in effect buy salvation both for themselves and for their departed loved ones.

These abuses of the penitential system brought about by the doctrine of purgatory led to calls for the reform of the Church. Martin Luther (1483–1546) was the first of the reformers to attack the sale of indulgences and other abuses in penitential practice. He was angered by the sale of these indulgences which he saw as little more than a fundraising exercise to increase the Church's wealth. Eventually all Protestants were to follow this lead and reject the view that penance was a sacrament instituted by Christ. Another reformer, John Calvin (1509–64), 'rejected the sacramental nature of penance because there was a lack of "matter" (the equivalent of water or bread and wine)',[3] though as we shall see later water *can* be used in this sacrament, recalling our baptism.

The Church of England retained confession as a kind of minor sacrament associated with spiritual growth. The Book of Common Prayer recognized the authority of the Church to hear confessions and to grant absolution, without providing a specific liturgical form for the reconciliation of a penitent. Provision was made for those who were unable to quieten their own consciences by the ministry of God's holy word to receive absolution, counsel and advice from a minister privately. Similar provision in the BCP 'The Order for the Visitation of the Sick' is also found, indicating its significance in the ministry of healing. During the Counter-Reformation the Roman Catholic Church eliminated the sale of indulgences and curbed other abuses, but has continued to maintain that private confession is a sacramental practice that came from Jesus himself.

## Modern liturgies

In most Christian churches modern liturgical celebrations of the eucharist begin with a penitential rite in which worshippers corporately confess their sins and ask for God's forgiveness. In the Church of England *Common Worship* rites the priest pronounces a general absolution over the congregation, normally in the form: 'Almighty God who forgives all who truly repent have mercy upon you, pardon and deliver you from all your sins.' In the Roman Catholic penitential rite of the mass, however, the prayer is in the precatory form of making a request: '*May* almighty God have mercy upon *us*, forgive *us* our sins.' This is because the indicative form of absolution declared by the priest, 'I absolve you from your sins', is traditionally reserved for private individual confession within the sacrament of reconciliation. It has sometimes been objected that the words 'I absolve you' are too sacerdotal, that is they attribute to the priest special or supernatural powers. This is to forget that the true minister of this sacrament is Christ himself, and that the words are no more sacerdotal than the words 'I baptize you in the name of . . .'

This sacrament has variously been called the sacrament of confession, penance and reconciliation, the latter being the more common modern usage. The term sacrament of cleansing or restoration has also been used. In the Roman Catholic and Orthodox Churches this sacrament has traditionally been seen to confer the forgiveness of sins committed after baptism. The new life received in Christian initiation has not abolished the frailty and weakness of human nature, nor the inclination to sin. What is needed when we sin is not to be re-baptized, but to be reminded of the baptism we have already undergone. This sacrament, therefore, is a reminder of our baptism.

*The Catechism of the Catholic Church* states:

> Christ instituted the sacrament of Penance for all sinful members of his Church; above all for those who, since Baptism, have fallen into grave sin, and have thus lost their baptismal grace and wounded ecclesial communion. It is to them that the sacrament of Penance offers a new possibility to convert and to recover the grace of justification. The Fathers of the Church present this sacrament as 'the second plank (of salvation) after the shipwreck which is the loss of grace.'[4]

I shall pick up this theme of the second plank, or second chance, later on.

Liturgical renewal took place in the Roman Catholic Church during the twentieth century and considerable changes were made to the Church's sacramental rites following the Second Vatican Council. The name of the sacrament of confession/penance was changed to reconciliation to emphasize the need to be reconciled not only with God but also with those we have hurt or offended (Matthew 5.23–26). A new rite was published in 1974 and in its introduction Pope Paul VI referred to it as a sacrament of healing: 'In order that this sacrament of healing may truly achieve its purpose amongst Christ's faithful, it must take root in their whole lives and move them to more fervent service of God and neighbour.'[5]

## The sacrament of penance and reconciliation

The introduction in the new Roman Catholic *The Rite of Penance* states:

> Our Saviour Jesus Christ, when he gave to his apostles and their successors power to forgive sins, instituted in his Church the sacrament of penance. Thus the faithful who fall into sin after baptism may be reconciled with God and renewed in grace. The Church 'possesses both water and tears: the water of baptism, the tears of penance'.[6]

In *The Rite of Penance* three forms of the rite have been devised. The primary one is the 'Rite for the Reconciliation of Individual Penitents', which is the norm for private confession. The second form is for use in a penitential church service with an opportunity for private confession within the service. The third form is rarely used and is for emergencies in which there is no time for private confession, for example when danger of death is imminent. These changes to the Roman Catholic rite have also prompted revisions in Anglican rites. However, the penitential rites and practices of Eastern and Orthodox Churches (which are not dealt with here) have remained fairly constant throughout history as they were unaffected by the Reformation that took place in the Western Church.

In 2006, as part of the new generation of liturgical provision in the Church of England, new services of 'Reconciliation and Restoration: Recovering Baptism' were published as part of the *Common Worship* 'Christian Initiation' rites. The underlying theology of these services is to 'provide individuals with routes back into the full baptismal life of the Christian community after separation through sin or as a result of sickness'.[7] They may be celebrated in a variety of ways, publicly in the community of faith or privately with individuals. The services provided are 'A Corporate Service of Penitence' (suitable for a diocesan, deanery or parish occasion) and two forms for 'The Reconciliation of a Penitent', for use 'when a person's conscience is burdened with a particular sin, when a person wishes to make a new beginning in the Christian life, or as a part of a regular personal discipline'.[8] The second form is linked particularly to an individual renewal of the baptismal covenant after sin.

## *Administration of the sacrament*

I now go on to describe in general terms how the rite of penance/reconciliation is administered to individuals within the Roman Catholic Church and the Church of England. For more specific detail the reader should consult the liturgical texts in each rite.

In the reconciliation of individual penitents the priest and penitent should first prepare themselves by prayer to celebrate this sacrament, the priest calling upon the Holy Spirit in order to receive enlightenment and charity. This is vital if the priest is to discern the deeper needs of the penitent.

In the Roman Catholic rite the priest welcomes the penitent, who makes the sign of the cross. If the penitent is unknown to the priest, the person indicates their state of life, the time of their last confession, their difficulties in leading the Christian life, etc. A text of holy scripture is then read which proclaims God's mercy and calls a person to conversion. In the Church of England rite, after the priest's welcome a short passage of scripture is read and the priest and penitent say together a prayer taken from the penitential verses of Psalm 51.

Following this, the penitent makes confession of his or her sins in the penitent's own words. The priest offers appropriate counsel or guidance to help the penitent begin a new life and encourages the penitent to make restoration. If the penitent has caused harm or scandal to others, the priest should lead the person to resolve to make appropriate restitution. The priest then imposes an act of penance on the penitent as a token of repentance. The penance should correspond to the seriousness and nature of the sins. The act of penance may take the form of prayer, self-denial or, especially, service to one's neighbour and works of mercy, or some other action as a sign of repentance. After this the penitent manifests his or her contrition and resolution to begin a new life by means of a prayer for God's pardon. Following this prayer of sorrow the priest lays hands on, or extends hands over, the head of the penitent and makes the sign of the cross when the absolution is pronounced. The essential words in the Roman Catholic rite are, 'I absolve you from your sins in the name of the Father, and of the Son, and of the Holy Spirit.' In the Church of England rite the absolution is chosen from one of six authorized versions ranging from the formula mentioned above to the prayer of absolution provided for the eucharist. In the Church of England rite the absolution may be made with water as a conscious recalling of baptism and the penitent may also make the sign of the cross with water in response to confession. The priest may, where appropriate, offer a ministry of prayer which may be accompanied by the laying on of hands and also anointing with the oil of healing. This may take place either before or after the absolution.

After receiving pardon for sins the penitent gives thanks in prayer for the mercy of God, following which in the Roman rite the penitent is dismissed with the words: 'The Lord has freed you from your sins. Go in peace.' In the Church of England rite the Lord's Prayer and a blessing may be said prior to the penitent being dismissed with the words 'the Lord has put away your sins'. The priest adds: 'Go in peace, and pray for me, a sinner too', for the clergy also take their place in the Church as a school for sinners and should have their own penitential discipline.

The sacrament of penance is ordinarily celebrated in a church. The Roman Catholic conferences of bishops have laid down that clearly visible confessionals are to be provided, equipped with a fixed screen between the penitent and the confessor. The traditional confessional box, however, is increasingly being replaced or supplemented by a reconciliation room with a table and two chairs set aside for an informal 'interview' style of confession. The confessional box is still preferred, however, by those who seek formality and anonymity. One Polish couple who came to St Marylebone for a while were horrified to learn that I hear confessions face to face in a small chapel and that people make an appointment to have their confession heard. Presumably in Poland they are used to queues of people in Roman Catholic churches waiting to go into a confessional box that is divided by a screen, so the priest probably does not know who the person is whose confession he is hearing. Confessional boxes are rarely seen in Anglican churches.

Both the Roman Catholic Church and the Church of England have rites for a corporate service of penitence, with an opportunity within the rite for the reconciliation of individual penitents. Provision for individual confession and absolution within these services is seen as a natural pastoral outworking of such corporate services.

During a Roman Catholic service of reconciliation several priests are required to be available in suitable places within the church to hear individual confessions and to reconcile the penitents. The introduction to the rite includes an opening prayer followed by the faithful listening together to the word of God. A homily is then given followed by a period of silence for examining one's conscience and awakening true sorrow for sins. The congregation then says a form of general confession, followed by joining in a litany or suitable song to express confession of sins and heartfelt contrition. Penitential intercessions take place including prayer for forgiveness and trust in God's mercy, concluding with the Lord's Prayer. Following the Lord's Prayer the priests go to the places assigned for hearing individual confession and may hear each other's confessions first before those of the congregation. The penitents who desire to confess their sins go to the priest of their choice. After receiving a suitable act of penance, penitents are absolved by the priest with the form used for the reconciliation of an individual penitent. When the confessions are over the presiding priest invites all to make an act of thanksgiving and to praise God for his mercy. This may be done in a hymn. The blessing and dismissal of the people follows.

In the Church of England a similar structure applies, though with some differences. Provision is made within the rite, for example, for the ministry of reconciliation of individual penitents to be accompanied by prayer and the laying on of hands and/or anointing with the oil of healing. The ministries of reconciliation and healing may take place either within the service or at its conclusion. A corporate service of penitence may lead into the celebration of the eucharist. Provision is also made, where there is no such celebration, for the rite to conclude with a thanksgiving for holy baptism in which the congregation may go in procession to the font and water may be sprinkled over the people.

The seasons of Advent and Lent are especially suitable for a penitential service and individual private confession, for those who feel the need for this sacrament usually make their confession before the great festivals of Christmas and Easter. In order to obtain the saving remedy of this sacrament, it is binding upon the faithful in the Roman Catholic Church to confess individually to a priest at least once a year every grave sin. Until a few years ago it was common practice in this country for Roman Catholics to go to sacramental confession prior to making their Sunday communion, and this practice still prevails to some extent in staunch Roman Catholic countries like Poland. Indeed, Pope Benedict XVI in his Apostolic Exhortation on the eucharist, *Sacramentum Caritatis*, comments that a love for the eucharist leads to a growing appreciation of the sacrament of reconciliation and the need to be in a state of grace in order to approach sacramental communion worthily.

## *'The Land of Beginning Again'*

Following this historical, theological and liturgical survey of the sacrament, we now visit a different landscape in which we will look at a number of pastoral considerations and situations. We have seen how this sacrament deals with the healing of our sins and how it is administered within the life of the Church. To be released from the power of sin is healing.

The healing power of forgiveness should never be underestimated. The head of a psychiatric hospital once said, 'I could dismiss half my patients tomorrow if they could be assured of forgiveness.' Forgiveness deals with the 'if onlys' in our lives. When we look back at some of the mistakes we've made and we say 'if only'. This sacrament of forgiveness deals with the skeletons we have locked away in the cupboard that we don't want other people to know about. A guilty conscience is a universal experience. It is said that the late Sir Arthur Conan Doyle, the creator of Sherlock Holmes, as a practical joke on 12 of the most respectable and famous people in this country sent a telegram to each of them saying, 'Fly at once, all is discovered.' Within 24 hours all 12 had fled the country. Oscar Wilde said in *The Ideal Husband*: 'Even you are not rich enough to buy back your past. No one is.'

Having looked at the formal liturgical provision for this sacrament, we shall be exploring in this section and the next the human experience that this sacrament was designed to meet. There is a deep-seated longing in the human psyche to leave behind the sin and failure of the past and begin again. This poem by Louisa Fletcher entitled 'The Land of Beginning Again' expresses this desire perfectly.

> I wish that there were some wonderful place
> Called the Land of Beginning Again,
> Where all our mistakes, and all our heartaches,
> And all our poor, selfish grief,

Could be dropped like a shabby old coat at the door
And never be put on again.

I wish we might come on it all unaware,
Like the hunter who finds a lost trail,
And I wish that the one whom all our blindness had done
The greatest injustice of all,
Could be at the gates like an old friend who waits
For the comrade he's gladdest to hail.

We'd find all the things we intended to do,
But forgot and remembered too late,
Little praises unspoken, little promises broken,
And all the thousand and one little duties neglected
That might have perfected the day for one less fortunate.

It wouldn't be possible not to be kind
In that Land of Beginning Again;
For the ones we misjudged, and the ones we grudged
Their moments of victory here
Would find in the grasp of our loving handclasp
More than penitent lips could explain.

For what had seemed hardest we'd find had been best,
And what had seemed loss had been gain;
For there isn't a thing that will not take wing,
If you face it and laugh it away;
And I think that the laughter is most what we're after,
In that Land of Beginning Again.

So I wish that there were some wonderful place
Called the Land of Beginning Again
Where all our mistakes, and all our heartaches,
And all our poor, selfish grief,
Could be dropped like a shabby old coat at the door
And never be put on again.

53

In the musical *Scrooge* the same sentiments are expressed in the song 'I'll Begin Again' (lyrics by Leslie Bricusse) after Scrooge has been brought to his senses about the miserly way he has lived his life:

I'll begin again,
I will build my life,
I will live to know that I've fulfilled my life.
I'll begin today, throw away the past,
and the future I build will be something that will last.

I'll begin again,
I will change my fate,
I will show the world that it is not too late.
I will never stop, while I still have time,
till I stand at the top of the mountain I must climb.

I will take the time I have left to live,
and I'll give it all that I have left to give.
I will live my days for my fellow men,
and I'll live in praise of that moment when
I was able to begin again.

I will start anew,
I will make amends,
and I'll make quite certain that the story ends
on a note of hope, on a strong amen,
and I'll thank the world and remember when
I was able to begin again.

I am sure that many of us have felt the force of these sentiments in our own lives.

Perhaps one of the most famous speeches on this theme was made by former US President Clinton at a prayer breakfast at the White House following his sexual relationship with Monica Lewinsky. Here is an extract from it, entitled in one newspaper 'There is no fancy way to say I sinned':

. . . I have asked all for their forgiveness. But I believe that to be forgiven, more than sorrow is required. At least two more things: first, genuine repentance, a determination to change and to repair breaches of my own making. I have repented. Second, what my Bible calls a broken spirit. An understanding that I must have God's help to be the person that I want to be. A willingness to give the very forgiveness I seek. A renunciation of the pride and the anger, which cloud judgment, lead people to excuse and compare and to blame and complain.

Now, what does all this mean for me and for us? First I will instruct my lawyers to mount a vigorous defence using all available, appropriate arguments. But legal language must not obscure the fact that I have done wrong. Second, I will continue on the path of repentance seeking pastoral support from caring people so that they can hold me accountable for my own commitment. Third, I will intensify my efforts to lead our country and the world toward peace and freedom, prosperity, and harmony. And in the hope that with a broken spirit and a still strong heart, I can be used for greater good for we have many blessings and many challenges and so much work to do . . . And if my repentance is genuine and sustained, and if I can then maintain both a broken spirit and a strong heart, then good can come of this for our country, as well as for me and my family. The children of this country can learn in a profound way that integrity is important and selfishness is wrong. But God can change us and make us strong at the broken places.

. . . A couple of days ago when I was in Florida, a Jewish friend of mine gave me this liturgy book called *Gates of Repentance*. And there was this incredible passage from a Yom Kippur liturgy and I would like to read it to you:

Now is the time for turning.
The leaves are beginning to turn from green to red to
    orange.
The birds are beginning to turn and are heading once
    more toward the south.
The animals are beginning to turn to storing their
    food for the winter.
For leaves, birds and animals, turning comes instinctively.
But for us, turning does not come so easily.
It takes an act of will for us to make a turn. It means
    breaking old habits.
It means admitting that we have been wrong, and this
    is never easy.
It means losing face. It means starting all over again.
    And this is always painful.
It means saying I am sorry.
It means recognising that we have the ability to change.
These things are terribly hard to do.
But unless we turn, we will be trapped forever in
    yesterday's ways.
Lord help us to turn from callousness to sensitivity,
    from hostility to love, from pettiness to purpose, from
    envy to contentment, from carelessness to discipline,
    from fear to faith.
Turn us around, O Lord, and bring us back toward you.
Revive our lives as at the beginning.
And turn us toward each other, Lord, for in isolation,
    there is no life.

Clinton's public remorse was certainly dramatic, even if there
were those who questioned his sincerity.

In a former parish of mine there was a young married
couple who sang in the choir. The wife regretfully had an affair
with another member of the choir. When the affair finally

ended, this young woman was desperate to repair the damage to her marriage and start again. Such was her sense of defilement that, having moved away with her husband, she was re-baptized in a Baptist church by total immersion, having been baptized already as a child in the Church of England. Her only way of coping spiritually was to be totally washed clean from head to foot and begin again. Baptism is a once-only sacrament, but I can understand what led her to want to be re-baptized.

The problem is that one cannot keep on being baptized every time one sins. What would happen if, God forbid, that person ever committed another major sin. The answer lies in this sacrament of penance and reconciliation, through which we begin again. Our baptism symbolizes death to the old life and rising to new life; but the day-to-day experience of Christians is also one of failure and sin, when we deny the reality of our new life and nature. That is why St Paul says: 'For I do not do the good I want, but the evil I do not want is what I do' (Romans 7.19). This is the contradiction at the heart of the life of every Christian, for we all know the place of failure in our lives. It is our response to this failure that determines whether we are left lame and destroyed, or whether we are strengthened and made whole. The choices are guilt or penitence. Guilt paralyses, cripples and destroys; penitence liberates. This is illustrated well in the gospels by Judas and Peter. Both went out from the presence of Jesus having failed, Judas in betrayal, Peter in denial. Peter went out and wept, that is, he confessed and repented; Judas went out and destroyed himself.

The Christian needs to live in the continual reality of being a forgiven sinner, a forgiveness that leads to freedom, release and healing – a starting again. I see entering the confessional as an entry into 'The Land of Beginning Again', where leaving the past behind we are cleansed from sin and can start anew. In God's eyes no one is damaged beyond repair.

## The second chance

Allied with the desire to begin again is the hope of a second chance in life, which is another basic human need that arises from time to time. Let us look at some examples of this.

In 1993 Jana Novotna lost to Steffi Graf in the women's tennis final at Wimbledon after throwing away an almost unassailable lead. Five years later she was to return to the Centre Court, this time to win the final. Following her triumph Simon Barnes wrote an article in *The Times* entitled 'Champion shows art of taking second chance'. Here is an extract:

> On Saturday Jana Novotna played a game of tennis for everyone who has ever made an absolute ghastly mistake, or to put it another way, the entire human race ... But there is, or there can be, such a thing as a second chance. Life is about a serial longing for the second chance; a chance to make amends, to others, to yourself. The most famous moment of Jana Novotna's life came with her Wimbledon disaster; the way she blew an unblowable lead in the final and sobbed on the shoulder of the Duchess of Kent ...
>
> It is the Wimbledon disaster we remember her for; the Wimbledon disaster that has made her beloved. And so she played for the principle that all of us hold so dear; that there can be a second chance, that a second chance, when offered, can be accepted. It is a subject close to everyone, but then I would think that. I have spent the past 18 months writing a novel on exactly that subject; the holiness of the second chance. That is why I, and that is why the Centre Court crowd, wanted Novotna to beat Nathalie Tauziat. That is why her wobbles caused even more pain than usual. That is why, when she served for the match and dropped her service, it was almost more than we could bear ... I have often seen the Centre Court filled with joy, with disappointment, with disbelief. I can't remember the place exploding with simple relief ... A second chance had

been offered and had been accepted. It was, in its way, an exquisite moment ... The blessedness of the second chance is such a universal principle that Novotna came out to play for us all. It was not, to be strictly accurate, all that much of a tennis match, but it was one of the great emotional occasions of the sporting year. We all of us blow golden chances in life; some of us get a second chance. The knack – perhaps the whole secret of life – is to take it.

An article in *The Times* (10 September 2001) included this comment about football: 'Second chances are rare and precious. In some moods, I am prepared to preach that the second chance is the most holy thing in life.' Not all footballers get second chances and the line between success and failure can be very thin. In the football World Cup final in Germany in 2006, who can forget how the career of the great French footballer Zinédine Zidane ended. This was his last game before retirement and could have marked the glorious climax to his dazzling career. He had already scored the first goal of the game. The match between France and Italy went into extra time and, with the scores level, Zidane rose majestically to head what looked like the winning goal, only for the Italian goalkeeper to pull off a brilliant save. What a story-book ending that would have been, had the ball hit the back of the net. However, minutes later in a moment of rage, Zidane was provoked into head-butting an opponent and was sent off in disgrace, an incident that may have cost his nation the World Cup. Zidane ruined his exit.

This incident exposed the tragic flaw in a football genius, one of the greatest footballers ever to grace the game. It is this exit for which he will now be remembered. An editorial in *The Times* (11 July 2006), headed 'Zidane joins the ranks of the fallen', commented: 'Ever since Adam was cast out of Paradise in the Fall man has had a fascination with the flawed fallen hero.' But as

Zidane's agent said: 'He is a human being, not a God.' For Zidane, the icon, there was to be no second chance. Nor was there for another sporting idol, Hans Cronje.

Cronje's downfall was even more dramatic than Zidane's. For six years he had been the greatly loved and respected South African cricket captain. He was a committed Christian, but foolishly became involved in a match-fixing scandal and was banned for life from playing professional cricket. He was later killed in a plane crash. His mother suggested that perhaps it was a blessing that her son had died, for he had suffered too much and lost all his confidence, she said, and would have had to bear the consequences of this scandal for the rest of his life. One cricket coach said that the whole tragedy was summed up for him by Cronje's mother suggesting that only in death could her son be freed from his burden.

An article on the second chance appeared in the *Church of England Newspaper* (7 August 2003) about the TV presenter John Leslie's fall from grace in the public eye following indecent assault charges of which he was acquitted. It was entitled 'A God of second chances'. It asked: 'how does he go about the rebuilding of a tarnished name, not just in his private life, but also the battle of winning over the public upon which his particular career depends? The court's verdict may be accepted but suspicion will continue based on the old adage that "there is no smoke without fire".' The article talked about the Church demonstrating that we know and serve a God of the second and third chances and more. It concluded: 'What John Leslie will need are people around him who are prepared to give him a second chance. People actually convicted of crimes also need those around them prepared to give them second chances. Those in our own churches and networks also need this. So, the challenge of the John Leslie story to us is whether we really believe in a God of the second chance or not.'

Fr Alan Fudge, a parish priest in a Roman Catholic church close to where I live once wrote this in his parish newsletter:

Dear Brothers and Sisters

All of us have a litany of regrets; things we regret having said or done; and things we regret not having said or done – but it is too late now. All of us have blotted our copybook at one time or another. And some of us think that the blot is black, massive and indelible. All of us have skeletons in our cupboard. And they can rattle at the most inconvenient time, covering us with shame and dread. For many of us there is something in our past life that we have to learn to live beyond: an event often connected with sin and guilt: a pregnancy outside marriage – an abortion – a broken vow – a trust that we betrayed – a relationship that broke up and for which we blame ourselves – a serious mistake we made against our parents, or children, or friends – an act of violence – a sexual indiscretion – a theft or lie that trapped us. Sometimes we think that the irrevocable has happened, giving us a sense of hopelessness. And we may fear that the rest of our life will be lived in the shadow and consequences of our mistake. We were given our chance in life, and we ruined it! Now we are being punished.

Is there another chance? A second chance? Can we rise above the past? For those who question and worry and doubt, the Word of God in the Liturgy today comes with a message of hope and salvation, a way forward. Look at King David, the adulterer, in the first reading. He has seduced Bathsheba and made her pregnant. He has arranged the killing of her husband, Uriah, and taken Bathsheba as his wife. Look at the 'woman with a bad name' in the Gospel. But David the adulterer is given the absolute assurance of forgiveness. And the woman with a bad name is allowed to have intimate contact with Christ, even to the point of covering his feet with her kisses. Most of us have adulterated areas of our lives. And most of us know that we also qualify for a 'bad name'. But the Good News proclaimed today is that we can take our place among the sinners and those with broken lives, and know that our many sins and mistakes are not for ever and ever and ever. We can be ransomed, healed, restored, forgiven! God gives us a second chance; and a third, and a fourth . . . And these other chances are as valid as the first. Nothing is irrevocable in our lives. Nothing. Because true Christianity does not teach us how to live. No! True Christianity teaches us how to live again and again and again.

It is interesting to read journalists in the secular press writing of the 'blessedness' and 'holiness of the second chance', and of the second chance being 'the most holy thing in life'. In the confessional we enter 'The Land of Beginning Again', where we receive 'the sacrament of the second chance' from the God of the second chance, who gives us more than one second chance in life through this sacrament of penance and reconciliation, in which we find healing and peace.

## *A sacrament of healing*

Having examined the human condition that gives rise to the need for this sacrament, we now look at the healing it can provide. The introduction to the Roman Catholic *The Rite of Penance* states that 'just as the wound of sin is varied and multiple in the life of individuals and of the community, so too the healing which penance provides is varied'.[9] The sacrament of penance is now seen as a sacrament of healing, bringing varied healing for the multiple wounds of sin, for sin is a disease that invades every aspect of our being. James 5.16 links healing and forgiveness: 'Therefore confess your sins to one another that you may be healed.' Confession of sins is the first step towards healing and wholeness, for forgiveness brings about inner healing which can also lead to physical healing, where sin and sickness are related in some way.

McManus comments:

> For the sin itself there is forgiveness. For the wound of sin there is healing. The wound of sin is an inner wound. The person is wounded in his or her self-esteem, self-image, relationships or memory . . . Confessors must become more sensitive to the presence of the wound of sin and more aware of the fact that in this sacrament they are not just ministers of God's pardon but also ministers of God's peace. Pardon is for the sin; peace is for the inner healing. In the prayer of absolution the priest exercises both ministries. He prays, 'Through the ministry of the Church may God give you pardon and peace.'[10]

Peace doesn't come in capsules and there are no short cuts to wholeness. As people go to confession regularly and are counselled and prayed for, they discover what their most recurring destructive weaknesses and feelings are that they need to be healed of. In sacramental confession the Holy Spirit can bring to light the root causes of the penitent's sin and the confessor (that is, the priest hearing the confession) is able to see what needs healing, especially if one sees the same confessor each time. Confession is particularly helpful in coming to terms with the past, and the sharing of our weaknesses, trials, temptations and sins can be a very healing experience.

It is true that some confession never leads to healing, particularly if one queues to go into the confessional box and then only a couple of minutes is available. Penitents always receive pardon and forgiveness through absolution of their sins, but they will not necessarily experience healing because they will need to be prayed for and counselled further, which ideally should be included within the sacrament of penance. The priest should pray for healing and strengthening after giving absolution.

McManus is concerned to ensure that there is time to pray and listen to the healing word of God within the administration of the sacrament. He states:

In my own experience as a confessor I have to say that when there was no celebration of the word of God, when there was no time spent in prayer with the penitent, when penitents were only interested in 'a quick absolution', I never witnessed any healing. This has led me to the strong conviction that sometimes absolution by itself is not enough. Absolution is essential to the celebration, but if the celebration is reduced, in a minimalist way, to absolution, we could have a deformation of the sacrament. Good liturgical time is needed for an integral celebration of the sacrament: time to listen; time to pray; time to share the sins that are on one's conscience; time to discern why those sins are there; time to make connections between the hurts and the wounds one has received and the manifestations of these in one's life. This kind of confession takes time and these deep needs normally are not met by a communal celebration.[11]

MacNutt comments that if I keep confessing the same sins time after time something is wrong: 'Either I don't really want to change and lack a purpose of amendment; or else I want to change but can't – in which case my sins are not voluntary and I can't in all honesty say I'm sorry. The answer here is, I think, that we need to add prayer for healing.'[12] He suggests the priest adds a simple prayer for healing directed at the problem area, either before or after giving absolution, though deep-seated addictions will require ongoing therapeutic support.

Sometimes people are adversely affected by hurts from the past, which even if not consciously remembered continue to affect their attitudes and behaviour today. These memories need to be identified and healed. In the healing of the memories, the memory is not necessarily wiped out, but its effects are no longer painful and debilitating. MacNutt recounts a fascinating story about inner healing of the memories:

I remember, in particular, praying for one woman in Peru who had a rather common problem; her life was altogether grey and dull. This boredom had nothing to do with her work; she was a missionary and liked her work. She knew that some kind of inner healing was necessary, for Christians should be filled with an abiding joy and zest for life. But you can't fake it either. So she spoke at length about all the things in her life that had caused her sadness. Nothing, however, was dramatic; all the events of her life seemed ordinary; there were no great crises. Usually when you listen to a person something turns on when you get the key to the healing; you feel in your heart, 'That's it; I know that's it.' But there was nothing like that. We prayed, then, as best we could, for all the wounding incidents of the past that she could think of. When the prayer was over, though, nothing changed. She experienced none of the peace, the joy, the lifting of the spirit that we have come to associate with a real inner healing.

The next day she came back and honestly admitted that nothing had happened. So again we (Mrs Barbara Shlemon and I) asked if she had thought of anything more we should pray for (often a person, out of shame, will omit the one incident that is the key to the inner healing). But she could think of nothing further. So we turned in prayer to the Lord for the light that would help us. While praying, Barbara received a mental picture of a young girl, about ten years old, holding a dog in her arms. Barbara said, 'This doesn't make sense, but let me tell you what I see.' The woman said that the picture brought something to mind she had forgotten: as a young girl of ten her best friend was her dog. But the dog was by then old and her parents took the dog away from her and 'put it out of its misery.' As an adult she had put this out of her mind; that's what you do to old dogs. But to a young girl it was as if her parents, the people she trusted most in life, had taken away her best friend and killed it. If you get hurt that painfully when you love a friend and trust people, maybe it's better not ever to trust or love that much again. So what she did as a little girl was to turn off, at it were, the flow of life, so that she would never again be hurt so deeply. What happened, though, was that she could never again experience joy or life either. Her protection kept her from experiencing either the joys or the sorrows of life.

So we prayed for what had happened to a ten-year-old girl. The next day I received this beautiful note: 'Life pours in. Rejoice! I feel so happy that I want to cry. This is the first time I have ever wanted to cry for being happy. Parts of my being are pulling back together.'[13]

Inside many of us lies a hidden world of suffering. The deepest wounds are those that are not visible to the eye. John Lennon, of Beatles fame, wrote in one of his songs: 'but one thing you can't hide is when you're crippled inside'. In the sacrament of penance, hidden things can be brought to light under the illumination of the Holy Spirit, and inner healing can take place. Thomas Merton stated, 'There is a hidden wholeness in us all.' The purpose of the prayer of faith in this sacrament is to find it.

## The sacrament in all but name

I went some years ago to a healing conference at which Francis MacNutt was speaking (he had been a Roman Catholic priest prior to his marriage to his wife Judith). MacNutt finished a teaching session on inner healing by telling the story of his wife when she was a young girl of ten (I hope I've remembered the details of the story correctly). She was very rotund. She was a jolly sort, but none of the boys ever took a liking to her because she was too fat. She liked one particular boy who was very popular. He was the mayor's son. All the girls liked him. One Valentine's Day she sent him a valentine card. She didn't buy it from a shop, she specially made it, and during class one day she passed it across the desks to him. The teacher caught her and didn't understand. She was very harsh and did a terrible thing: she got Judith to stand up in front of the class and read out the card. Judith pleaded with her teacher but to no avail. After the bell went for the end of the lesson she ran into the toilet and cried her eyes out.

As she was coming out of the toilet she overheard three boys talking, who didn't see her. One of them was the mayor's son and the other two were taking the mickey out of him. In order to try and get himself off the hook he said to the other two: 'How could anyone like Judith, she is so fat and ugly?' From that moment on she disliked her body. In the changing rooms she hid in a corner. Even in later life when she was no longer fat, she was still ashamed of her body. Jesus had to heal her inside.

Francis MacNutt closed the meeting. The lights were dimmed in the auditorium and 2,000 people sat there in silence as he left the stage to allow God to do his work. Then from the silence sobs could be heard from people all over the auditorium. Silence punctuated by sobs. Sobs as people's wounds and hurts were being healed by God. Those of us who were not in tears left the auditorium for a refreshment break before the next session. When I returned to the auditorium 15 minutes later, there was a young man standing at the front shrieking; prolonged shrieking, punching the air and shouting, 'I'm healed! I'm healed! I'm healed!'

All around the auditorium others were sobbing and being prayed for and counselled by those next to them, as people were coming to terms with their past and its effect on their present. Many of these hurts would have been caused by sin in some way. The scene was as if a penitential service of reconciliation had taken place and these were now the impromptu individual confessions being heard, with prayer for healing. It wasn't the sacrament of reconciliation in a liturgical sense, but nevertheless God's grace was being imparted as though it was – 'confess your sins to one another, and pray for one another, so that you may be healed' (James 5.16).

## *Why auricular confession?*

It is reported that in one church a new priest arrived who was rather deaf. Unfortunately, because people tend to whisper in the confessional box, he couldn't hear their confessions very well. So parishioners were asked to write their sins on pieces of paper and pass them over. This worked quite well until one woman handed him a slip bearing the list, '$^1/_2$lb tea, $^1/_2$lb butter, 2lb sugar, $^1/_2$lb cheese'. The priest passed it back, and the woman realized that she had left her list of sins with the grocer.

Auricular confession is the name we give to the act by which the penitent confesses their sins to God in the presence of a priest as confessor who then grants absolution. This ministry of reconciliation is an extension of Jesus' own ministry and, as we have seen, is the means by which the Church mediates the grace of God's forgiveness to those who turn from their sins. It should be noted that there are no general absolutions anywhere in the gospels. Each individual stands before God alone.

Non-sacramental confession can be a very subjective experience. When we confess our sins in our private prayers or during a Sunday service, we are saying them to a God who is largely made in our own image and who has comfortably accepted our sins. It can be as though we are imagining we are confessing our sins to God, but in fact we are confessing them only to ourselves. It is what Dietrich Bonhoeffer described as 'self-forgiveness' rather than 'real forgiveness'. Sacramental confession, however, can be liberating. He states:

> In confession a man breaks through to certainty. Why is it that it is often easier for us to confess our sins to God

than to a brother? . . . We must ask ourselves whether we have not often been deceiving ourselves with our confession of sin to God, whether we have not rather been confessing our sins to ourselves and also granting ourselves absolution . . . Who can give us the certainty that, in the confession and the forgiveness of our sins, we are not dealing with ourselves but with the living God? God gives us this certainty through our brother. Our brother breaks the circle of self-deception . . . A man who confesses his sins in the presence of a brother knows that he is no longer alone with himself; he experiences the presence of God in the reality of the other person.[14]

In the presence of a priest our sins no longer appear comfortable but cause us pain as we confess them; and so they should, for they are not a private affair but have affected others, and the pain we feel should lead us to do something about them. Our sins are not being confessed to a priest but to God in the presence of the priest acting as his representative, who is then able to give advice. This advice will be sounder than the advice we receive from a friend, because in the confessional we should tell the priest everything, whereas with others we tend to edit what we tell them and cut bits out. In the confessional, however, the priest should get the full picture and be able to advise more soundly as a result. This spiritual undressing in front of a priest should be compared to that of undressing for a doctor's physical examination. Neither is embarrassed, for both have seen many people like us before. This sacrament is the one place where we can come and not make excuses. It is the one place where we no longer need to hide, reversing the process of Genesis 3.8 where the man and his wife hid themselves after having done wrong.

It's not just the sins of *commission* that we need forgiveness for – the wrong actions we've committed. It's also the sins of *omission* – things that we didn't do. That's why the general confession in the Book of Common Prayer includes both types of sin: 'We have left undone those things which we ought to have done, And done those things which we ought not to have done, And there is no health in us.'

Sacramental confession has an especially valuable part to play in the comfort of the terminally ill and dying where one's conscience is particularly acute. Oscar Wilde is reported to have said on his deathbed: 'How else but through a broken heart may the Lord Christ enter in.' Our conscience can also be misinformed, so that in auricular confession the priest has the opportunity to assist the penitent to see things accurately. An example of this may be where someone is plagued by a particular temptation and is consumed with guilt because of it. What may not have been realized is that temptation is not sin, for even our Lord was tempted in all things like we are, but without sin (Hebrews 4.15). It is the yielding to the temptation that is the sin and so the penitent may be persecuting himself or herself unnecessarily.

There is a story of a girl making her confession to a priest, saying jokingly, 'Father, I've committed the most terrible sin.' He said, 'What is it?' 'Well, I look into the mirror and I say to myself every day, "Molly, you're the prettiest girl in the world."' The priest looked at her for a moment or two and said, 'Molly, that's not a terrible sin, that's just a terrible mistake.'

Needless to say, confession is not magic. We don't automatically receive the grace of this sacrament regardless of our disposition. To receive its full benefit we have to thoroughly prepare ourselves, to be truly sorry for our sin and desire to avoid it in the future. The rear of the clergy house where I live faces the mews house of the famous rock star Noel Gallagher of Oasis. His dustbin is outside the front of his house and late one evening while he was out I watched as two young women emptied the contents of the dustbin onto the mews and sifted through the rubbish to see what they could find. Who'd be a pop idol! This sacrament is about sifting through the rubbish to be disposed of in our lives with the assistance of another person. Who has not felt spiritually lighter and less burdened as they walk away from this sacrament after receiving absolution? It is as though the refuse collector has come and removed the rubbish.

Confession can, of course, be misused. Rather than revealing ourselves to the confessor we can do the opposite. George Hacker, in his book *The Healing Stream*, comments: 'I have heard confessions in which nothing that really mattered was given away, and when I began to probe gently, the person concerned quickly moved on to someone else.'[15]

Confession is linked to counsel, advice and spiritual direction. Increased emphasis is now placed on confession as a means of reconciliation, healing and spiritual growth and may form part of a wider discussion covering a range of personal issues. This discussion increasingly takes place in a more informal face-to-face pastoral setting, in which the penitent kneels only for the liturgical prayers of confession and absolution. The confessor may suggest that the penitent could benefit from a session with a trained counsellor or a spiritual director, though some feel that confession and spiritual direction should be kept separate. Confession always needs to be distinguished from counselling because confession concludes with absolution and the reassurance that the penitent's sins are forgiven by God.

The sacramental seal of confession is also absolutely inviolate. The priest is never permitted to disclose to anyone else what he has heard in confession, unlike the risk one runs when revealing one's inner self to friends. The seal cannot be broken under any circumstances, including after the death of the penitent. Neither does the confession of sin affect the relationship between priest and penitent, as though the confessor is always remembering the penitent's sins every time they meet. My memory is so bad that I'm lucky to remember the person's name, let alone their sins! Besides, I'm very much a sinner too. All of us would probably echo Barbra Streisand's words: 'If God wrote my biography I wouldn't like it.'

Another aspect of sacramental confession, which distinguishes it from other forms of confession or counsel, is the act of penance imposed on the penitent by the priest, which helps the reconciliation process. Penance is the historic name given to the rite that is now normally called the sacrament of reconciliation. Penance is that part of the rite where, in order that the penitent show true sorrow for their sin, the priest imposes a penance, some appropriate action of contrition and reparation before absolution is given. I find the following fictional story of Tommy O'Shaughnessy's visit to the confessional box rather amusing:

'Bless me Father, for I have sinned. I have not been to confession for six months. On top of that, I've been with a loose woman.' The priest sighs. 'Is that you, little Tommy O'Shaughnessy?' 'Yes, Father, 'tis I.' 'And who might be the woman you were with?' 'I shan't be tellin' you, Father. It would ruin her reputation.' 'Well, Tommy, I'm bound to find out sooner or later, so you may as well tell me now. Was it Brenda O'Malley?' 'I cannot say.' 'Was it Patricia Fitzgerald?' 'I'll never tell.' 'Was it Lisa O'Shanter?' 'I'm sorry, but I'll not name her.' 'Was it Cathy O'Dell?' 'My lips are sealed.' 'Was it Fiona Mallory?' 'Please, Father, I cannot tell you.' The priest sighs in frustration. 'You're a steadfast lad, Tommy O'Shaughnessy, and I admire that. But, you've sinned and you must do penance.' The priest then imposes a penance for Tommy to undertake. Tommy walks back to his pew. His friend Sean slides over and whispers, 'What did you get?' 'Five more good leads!' says Tommy.

Undertaking penance is an important part of the restorative process. The confessor will make the penance fit the sin, for instance a devotional act, a Bible reading, performing some practical act of kindness. Someone whose major sin is pride will need to undertake something that will induce humility, a person who is lazy will need a penance that encourages activity. In Luke's gospel (Luke 19.8) Zacchaeus made financial restitution to those he had defrauded. As the Roman Catholic *The Rite of Penance* states: 'Penance always entails reconciliation with our brothers and sisters who are always harmed by our sins.'[16]

Jonathan Baker, in his booklet *How Forgiveness Works*, comments: 'Something decisive and objective must underlie our concept of forgiveness if it is to have any real transforming power. "Can't you forgive me?" implores the adulterous central character in Tom Wolfe's novel, *Bonfire of the Vanities*. "I suppose I could," replied his wife. "But what would that change?"'[17] True conversion is completed by acts of penance and amendment of life that show the sincerity of our contrition and reinforce the healing process.

The priest asks the penitent to perform an act that is a practical expression of his or her penitence, but this should not be construed as a way of 'earning' forgiveness. It is not as though specific acts of penance somehow make up for wrongs committed. Rather, that as a key part of the ongoing process of restoring relationships with God and with others, these acts of penance provide a wholesome discipline that allows the healing process to continue, much as in the same way that someone who has broken a leg undertakes ongoing physiotherapy once the plaster is off, until normal use returns. Christian penance is, therefore, part of a process that is initiated and sustained by God's healing grace, and is not to be seen as an act through which we can somehow atone for our sins.

## Decline in use

In recent years the use of the confessional by Roman Catholics and others has been in steady decline. There are probably a number of reasons for this. One cannot be that people go to confession less today because they are sinning less. It is more that people have lost the awareness of how destructive sin is. Another reason is that in a former age people lived in fear of judgement and eternal damnation, although this belief is not quite dead. In the church school in my last parish a teacher said to a mother, 'Michael's been much better behaved today.' The proud mother replied, 'Yes, we've told him that if he's naughty Jesus will see him and throw a brick at his head.'

It used to be that people would also go to the priest to get things off their chest, whereas now they are more likely to go to a counsellor or psychotherapist who offer alternative 'non-judgemental' therapy. If they go to the priest, it is more for moral guidance or assurance of God's forgiveness. The practice of confession is helpful, however, because it brings penitents into an environment of love, understanding and acceptance in which they can accept the truth about themselves without being psychologically threatened, and which enables them to accept God's forgiveness because they are enabled to forgive themselves.

Many Christians outside the Catholic tradition have tended to have a jaundiced view towards confession. In the nineteenth century, priests who heard confessions in the Church of England could find themselves locked out of their churches and deprived of their livings for fear of popery. All this meant that in Victorian England, while sin was constantly talked and preached about, people often did not experience personal forgiveness of sins.

Morton, an evangelical Anglican priest, wrote a booklet entitled *Personal Confession Reconsidered* after discovering for himself God's forgiveness and healing through this sacrament. He comments: 'One difficulty that arises from the current situation is that Anglicans who want to make their Confession often find it difficult to find clergy willing to hear it. It is to be hoped therefore that ministers will not shy away from this area, but will recognise the value it has and the spiritual benefits it offers their congregations.'[18]

John Colwell, a Baptist pastor and lecturer in Christian doctrine, comments in his book *Promise and Penance*:

I cannot help but wonder how many spiritual disasters (some of them highly public) may have been averted had some formal discipline of spiritual direction and confession been in place . . . it is high time some Evangelical ministers abandon delusory notions of themselves as senior managers or spiritual entrepreneurs and rediscovered the responsibilities of pastoral care, of the 'cure of souls'.[19]

This is an appropriate place to tell another no doubt fictional story. A mother of naughty twin boys was complaining to another mother about the problems she was experiencing trying to discipline her two boys. The other mother, who also had two sons, said she had solved the problem by taking her sons to church for confession. After one incident of particularly bad behaviour, the mother of the twins decided to try her friend's remedy and took her sons along to the confessional. The first boy met the priest and was taken into the confessional and the priest went round to the other side. The priest asked the boy, 'Where is God?' The boy was trembling so much he was unable to reply. Once again the priest asked, 'Where is God?' Terrified, the boy rushed out, grabbed his brother and they ran as fast as they could until they could run no further. The other brother asked, 'What happened?' Gasping, his brother replied, 'They've lost God, and now they're blaming us!'

Unfortunately, many Protestant clergy have 'lost God', as it were, when it comes to offering people this sacrament. Colwell comments, 'Without some sacramental dynamic of continuing forgiveness and restoration the Church lacks visible sacramental discipline and a Church lacking discipline is a Church lacking credibility.'[20] However, I have met several Anglican clergy whose churches are involved in the charismatic movement, who have informed me that they hear more confessions now than they have ever heard before (although they may be less liturgical), as spiritual renewal has opened up deep-seated needs in people. The traditional Anglican position towards confession has been summed up in the words: 'All may, some should, none must.'

It is a pity that in recent years many have turned their backs on this sacrament, thereby depriving themselves of an important means of healing. One of the most moving invitations to individual sacramental confession that I have come across was again to be found in one of Fr Alan Fudge's newsletters to his parishioners on the theme of the Sunday gospel that week, which was the story of the prodigal son in Luke 15.11–24:

Dear Brothers and Sisters,
'He left for a distant country . . .' The journey made by the 'prodigal son' in the famous Gospel passage is a journey we have all made. All of us know what it is to live in a country very distant from God and very distant from the Church. Some of us leave 'our Father's house' and visit this country so often and so regularly that we can almost claim dual nationality – we are schitzo.

The prodigal son found himself feeding pigs. Is there anything more degrading for a Jewish boy than to feed pigs? Most of us have had our fair share among the swine. This distant country is, of course, the scene of our sins. Sins of envy and lust; sins of selfishness and laziness; sins of gluttony and drink, and over-indulgence in many other things too. And we know that in this distant country the bright lights are not bright for too long. And the fleshy pleasures that attract us there can soon turn putrid. They can stink. They can ooze pus. But in the face of all our distant journeying; of our moral and sexual chaos; of the emotional mess; of our cynicism and indifference; of our perseverance in sin; God our Father remains faithful.

God is not shocked or scandalised by our sins. Seeing us in this distant country he is filled with compassion and moved to pity. He waits and longs for our return. He never gives up the hope of welcoming us back. He is hopelessly prejudiced in our favour. We have only to glance in his direction; only to feel the first stirrings of regret or shame, and he immediately goes out to meet us. Even if we are still a very long way off, and the smell of the pig sty still clings to our clothes and our body, still he goes out to meet us. For those who can say: 'I have sinned against heaven and against you', there is a royal welcome. Robe, ring and sandals are prepared and a celebration is made ready.

Where can we experience this welcome? Where can we be embraced by a loving father? Where can we taste the mercy and love of God and find peace? Where? In the Sacrament of Penance. In the simple and humble confession of our sins. No one need be ashamed of the visits he has made, or the time he has spent in the distant country. Come to this sacrament. Make your confession. Then you will find peace.

## Forgive and be forgiven

In order to receive the forgiveness of God in this sacrament, we need to be ready to forgive others. Forgiveness is not restricted to our relationship with God, but spills out into our relationship with others. In the Lord's Prayer we ask God to 'forgive us our sins as we forgive those who sin against us'. This is reinforced at the end of the Lord's Prayer in Matthew 6.14 where Jesus says: 'For if you forgive others their trespasses, your heavenly Father will also forgive you; but if you do not forgive others, neither will your Father forgive your trespasses.' Divine and human forgiveness go hand in hand. When John Wesley approached General Oglethorpe on behalf of a convict, to plead for the prisoner, the General said to John Wesley, 'I never forgive.' John Wesley replied, 'Then I hope, Sir, that you never sin.'

Jesus underlined and illustrated this principle that a person must forgive in order to be forgiven in the parable of the unforgiving slave (Matthew 18.23–35), where a king wished to settle accounts with his slaves. One owed him 10,000 talents, and as he could not pay the king ordered him and his family and their possessions to be sold. The slave begged for time to pay. Out of pity the lord forgave him his debt. The same slave, however, came upon one of his fellow slaves who owed him only 100 denarii. He seized him by the throat and demanded payment. His fellow slave begged for time to pay, but he was refused and thrown into prison until he should pay the debt. The other slaves were distressed and reported this to the lord who summoned the unjust slave saying, 'I forgave you all that debt because you pleaded with me. Should you not have had mercy on your fellow slave as I had mercy on you?' In his anger the lord handed him over to be tortured until he should pay the entire debt. Jesus concludes, 'So my heavenly Father will also do to every one of you if you do not forgive your brother or sister from your heart.'

God's willingness to forgive is conditional upon our willingness to forgive others. We cannot expect to receive forgiveness if we are unwilling to offer it. That is why St Augustine called this petition in the Lord's Prayer 'the terrible petition'. St John Chrysostom, Bishop of Antioch in the fourth century, tells us that people of his day wanted to remove this clause from the Lord's Prayer. C. S. Lewis said that everyone thinks forgiveness is a lovely idea until they have something to forgive. An American hostage in Iran was asked on television after his release if he'd ever go back to Iran. 'Yes,' he replied, 'in a B52 bomber.'

An article in *The Times* (22 March 2006) by Carol Midgley, following the murder of black Liverpool teenager Anthony Walker by white racists, highlighted his mother Gee's willingness and ability to forgive:

> Gee Walker was leaving the crown court room, where she had just forced herself to listen to the hideous forensic

detail of how her son had been murdered with an axe, when somebody slipped her a note. It was from Paul Taylor, the racist thug who had buried the blade in Anthony's skull and ended his life. The letter said that he was sorry. If Taylor had written it hoping for Mrs Walker's forgiveness, he was too late. She had already forgiven him, just as she had forgiven his accomplice Michael Barton. 'I cannot hate. I have to forgive them. Hate is what killed Anthony,' she said after Taylor, 20 and Barton 17 were jailed for Anthony's murder. 'Their minds must be very tortured.' The magnanimity of this gesture took the nation's breath away . . . To her, it is obvious that if she did not forgive, and did not answer racism and hate with tolerance and love, it would insult the memory of Anthony who, like her, lived by the tenets of peace and Christianity.

While it is easy to put Mrs Walker's ability to forgive down to the fact that she is a practising Christian, not all Christians are able to do so. The most high-profile case of this recently was that of the Revd Julie Nicholson, who resigned as Priest-in-Charge of St Aiden's Church in Bristol because she could not forgive the 7/7 bombers who killed her daughter Jenny, aged 24, in a London tube train. Jenny studied at the Royal Academy of Music opposite the church where I am the Rector and sometimes used the church for performances. Her mother Julie has gained a certain fame as 'the priest who can't forgive'. She commented, 'It's very difficult to stand behind an altar and lead people in words of peace and reconciliation and forgiveness when I feel very far from it myself. So for the time being, that wound in me is having to heal.' She went on, 'I have laid forgiveness to one side and it's for God at the moment. It's beyond my human capacity to deal with. And I don't feel that's outrageous, unbelievable or even un-Christian.'

Many sympathized with her, for not everyone sees forgiveness as necessary or even desirable. An article in the *Daily Mail* carried the headline 'A pastor's God-given right not to forgive'. Minette Marrin wrote an article in *The Times* on Easter Day 2006 headed 'Forgiveness is an inhuman quality'. She stated:

> Forgiveness may be divine but I don't think it is human. To me it seems either pointless or meaningless . . . If someone dashed my baby's brains again the wall, laughing, or cut my children's arms off, I would think my forgiveness completely irrelevant. I might come to understand why it happened. I might come to terms with it somehow. I might put aside any feelings of vengeance. But either the wrongdoers could not really help what they were doing – they were themselves the victims of terror, superstition, abuse or madness and were not fully responsible for their actions – or else they were fully responsible and did it anyway. Forgiveness doesn't seem to me to apply.

But for Gee Walker forgiveness is central to her own survival following the murder of her son. 'In a way I'm not doing it for them, I'm doing it for me,' she said. 'Unforgiveness is a heavy weight. It's a big load to carry. I've seen what it does to people. They become bitter, angry. I don't want to be like that. I don't want to be a victim twice over.'

Most of us would hope that our capacity to forgive is not so tested. A former chaplain of our secondary school at St Marylebone is the daughter of a one-time bishop in Iran. Her brother Bahram was murdered over there, shot through the head at point blank range. Gunmen on a previous occasion had tried to kill the bishop but failed, so they took the life of his son instead. It was not safe for the bishop to attend his own son's funeral. The bishop's wife standing beside the coffin at the funeral of her son, said this:

> Bahram belonged to God and we now yield him back to him. For 24 years he was a blessing and a joy to us and without doubt he has given his life in place of his father

. . . I will never understand how anyone could be so callous as to cut off the life of a young man so brutally, but we believe that God will take this wicked and senseless act and use it to bring blessing and strength to his Church. We know the life of Bahram will not remain without fruit and we yield him to God and his Church. The night that this happened the prayer for that day in my little book of prayers was this – 'O God, forgive our enemies and those who oppress us, and never allow a spirit of revenge and hatred to remain within us.' God Himself was our example in this when Jesus prayed on the cross – 'Father forgive them for they know not what they do.'

In one parish I was asked to visit a woman at her home to pray for the healing of her legs, which were hugely swollen, and which had meant that she had been unable to walk to church for many weeks. I gave her holy communion on several occasions and prayed for her healing without success. During my visits I learnt that this woman had not spoken to her daughter for several years, in fact since her daughter had given birth to a child out of wedlock (although she did marry the father later). At the time this was a disgrace for her mother, a sin for which she just couldn't forgive her daughter.

I was to discover, however, that this woman herself had never been married, and her daughter had been conceived as a result of an affair she had when she was young. She couldn't forgive her daughter for being in the very same situation she had been in. I visited the daughter and a reconciliation was brought about with her mother, prayer for forgiveness and absolution was offered and shortly afterwards this woman was physically restored and back in church. The liturgy of the Church in the Lord's Prayer petitions God to 'forgive us our sins as we forgive those who sin against us', and James 5.16 states: 'confess your sins to one another, and pray for one another, so that you may be healed'.

81

I am not necessarily inferring a link between bodily ill-health and lack of forgiveness in this particular story. It would appear, however, that in the story of the healing of the paralytic in Mark 2.1–12, for example, healing and forgiveness are linked, for Jesus forgave him his sins before telling him to get up and walk. Because of the close interrelationship between our bodies and our emotional and spiritual health, some physical sicknesses do clear up when the roots of unforgiveness, anxiety, resentment, bitterness and so on are removed through a ministry of prayer and reconciliation. Some illnesses have psychosomatic causes, for a sick mind can produce a sick body. The receiving of forgiveness and the act of forgiving others can in some cases open the way to healing and wholeness. That is why this particular sacrament of healing is so important and why its use should be encouraged.

# 4

## The sacrament of the eucharist

—•◆•—

We come now to the precious jewel in the sacramental crown, the holy eucharist. It may have been noted, by those who hold to there being seven sacraments in the life of the Church, that apart from the three healing sacraments under consideration the others normally only take place once in a lifetime. Indeed, only the sacrament of the eucharist is celebrated regularly by most Christians, usually weekly but daily by some. In examining the sacrament of the eucharist we shall see that it is held by many Christians to be the 'source and summit of the Christian life' and 'the healing service *par excellence*'. We begin with consideration of its biblical origins.

### Biblical background

The origins of the eucharist are to be found in contemporary Jewish meal customs, with the blessings offered over food before and after a meal and in particular the bread and wine at family meals on the Sabbath and at the Passover. The Greek word 'eucharistia' (thanksgiving) is a translation of the Hebrew 'berakah', the term which denotes this blessing. Jesus' last supper (whether a Passover or fellowship meal) had included a full meal, as well as the bread and wine to which he attached particular meaning. We do not know when the full meal disappeared, but by the end of the first century the eucharist was no longer celebrated in connection with a meal.

The New Testament gives us quick glimpses of first-century eucharists. At the Last Supper, Christ identified bread and wine with his body and blood (see Matthew 26.26–29; Mark 14.22–25; Luke 22.15–20; 1 Corinthians 11.23–26). In a later age a range of interpretations was to be put on Christ's words 'This is my body/blood', ranging from 'This *becomes* my body/blood' to 'This *represents* my body/blood'. Although the fourth gospel has no narrative account of this eucharistic institution, John 6 explains the meaning of the eucharist in the discourse on Jesus as the bread of life, and some would cite John 6.51 as a definitive statement of Christ's presence in the eucharistic bread: 'the bread that I will give for the life of the world is my flesh'. John's account of this Capernaum sermon has Jesus also saying: 'I tell you, unless you eat the flesh of the Son of Man and drink his blood, you have no life in you. Those who eat my flesh and drink my blood have eternal life, and I will raise them up on the last day; for my flesh is true food and my blood is true drink. Those who eat my flesh and drink my blood abide in me, and I in them' (6.53–56).

In 1 Corinthians 10.16–17 St Paul records: 'The cup of blessing that we bless, is it not a sharing in the blood of Christ? The bread that we break, is it not a sharing in the body of Christ?' This clarifies the meaning of Paul's narrative account of the institution of the eucharist in 1 Corinthians 11.23–26. St Paul continues in verses 27–30:

> Whoever, therefore, eats the bread or drinks the cup of the Lord in an unworthy manner will be answerable for the body and blood of the Lord. Examine yourselves, and only then eat of the bread and drink of the cup. For all who eat and drink without discerning the body, eat and drink judgment against themselves. For this reason many of you are weak and ill, and some have died.

Some regard the sacrilege as treating the bread as ordinary bread. Others take a wider view of the word 'body' being the

Church as the body of Christ and therefore the word 'discerning' as referring to the state of our relationships with other Christians. Nevertheless there is an identification to be made between the act of communion and the presence of Christ.

From New Testament times there has always been a fear of unworthy communion, based on St Paul's attribution of sickness and death among Corinthian communicants to this cause (1 Corinthians 11.30). But the fear was attached not to the elements themselves but to receiving them unworthily and so being guilty of profaning the body and blood of the Lord (11.27). This sickness could be important, as we shall see later on, for our understanding of the eucharist as a healing sacrament. There may be other allusions to the eucharist in the New Testament, in the gospel accounts of the miraculous multiplication of loaves and fishes and possible allusions also in Hebrews and Revelation.

In view of the sacrificial overtones that became attached to the eucharist in post-biblical times we should perhaps note here the biblical background to this sacrificial language. In the ancient world offerings were made to deities to appease their anger or win their blessing and it was from within this cultural milieu that the Jewish sacrificial system emerged. These sacrifices included thank offerings of grain, oil or wine and sin offerings, in which the death of an unblemished lamb or other animal had particular significance, especially as the shedding of its blood was seen to make atonement or reconciliation with God for sins committed (Leviticus 17.11).

Jesus himself at the Last Supper associated his death with the Passover, at which the Passover lambs were slaughtered, and the making of a new covenant with God. The first Christians expressed their conviction that through the life and death of Jesus Christ they were reconciled to God. St Paul writes of Christ as an atoning sacrifice and in 1 Corinthians 5.7 states that 'our Paschal lamb, Christ, has been sacrificed. Therefore, let us celebrate the festival.' However, nowhere does he link the feast itself with the Lord's supper.

It was inevitable, however, that eventually sacrifice came to be focused on the eucharist, for Hebrews 13.15 speaks of liturgical worship as offering up to God 'a sacrifice of praise', and 1 Peter 2.5 speaks of the task of the Christian community being to offer up 'spiritual sacrifices'. St Paul also spoke of Christians presenting their bodies 'as a living sacrifice, holy and acceptable to God, which is your spiritual worship' (Romans 12.1). While the eucharist, therefore, came to be regarded as a 'sacrifice of praise' and a 'spiritual sacrifice' by those early Christians, it was not repeating the once-for-all sacrifice of Christ upon the cross, for 'Christ has offered for all time a single sacrifice for sins' (Hebrews 10.12).

## Church history

The emerging Christian community met daily in believers' homes as well as in borrowed rooms of public buildings for such activities as preaching, teaching, prayer, healing and the breaking of bread, which was probably a meal incorporating the eucharist (see Acts 2.42, 46). Amanda Porterfield, in her book *Healing in the History of Christianity*, comments: 'Healing was part of the Eucharist from the beginning. Early Christians anticipated bodily resurrection through participation in fellowship with Christ during the Eucharistic meal, and physical healings in the course of the meal were not unusual.'[1] St Ignatius of Antioch (*c.* 112) referred to the eucharistic elements as 'the medicine of immortality'.

An early eucharistic liturgy, possibly dating from *c.* 200, 'The Liturgy of St Mark' from the Patriarchate of Alexandria, contains these words in the anaphora (eucharistic prayer):

> Visit, Lord, the sick among your people and in mercy and pity heal them. Drive away from them and from us every disease and illness; expel the spirit of weakness from them.

Raise up those who have lain in lengthy illnesses, heal those that are troubled by unclean spirits . . . And also, Lord, heal the diseases of our souls, and cure our bodily weaknesses, healer of souls and bodies.[2]

The early Church fathers were unequivocal in their belief that what is received in the breaking of bread or communion is the body and blood of Christ. By the fourth century Cyril, Bishop of Jerusalem (315–86) is using a prayer (epiclesis) that asks the Father to send the Holy Spirit upon the bread and wine, in order that they may be changed into the body and blood of Christ, a practice that the churches of the east were to follow. In the west, Ambrose, Bishop of Milan (334–97) was suggesting that it was the recitation of Jesus' words of institution that accomplished the consecration or change in the elements, which the churches of the west were to hold to. Today the whole eucharistic prayer is seen to be consecratory, which includes both actions.

As well as a heightened emphasis of the real presence of Christ in the sacrament brought about by a change taking place to the bread and wine, there was a corresponding sacrificial development. In the sacrificial climate of the first Christian centuries it was essential for the Church to have a sacrifice if it was to have any validity in the eyes of its members and potential converts, and so the eucharist increasingly came to be seen as not just the offering of a sacrifice of praise and thanksgiving, but as a sacrifice to obtain forgiveness of sins and other benefits. St Cyril taught that great benefit was derived by those for whom prayer was offered while the 'holy and most terrifying sacrifice' was set forth before God upon the altar.

Alongside these theological developments, architectural changes were also taking place. In the Constantine era in the first part of the fourth century, when Christianity moved towards becoming the state religion, a considerable church-building programme took place which saw the emergence of the basilica as a replacement for the house church, and Christian worship moved from the home to the 'palace'. Magnificent churches were built over the next centuries to cope with the growing numbers.

In the fifth century the Christians in Rome began to take the bodies of saints from the catacombs and other burial sites and place them in churches within the city. The multiplication of relics in a church building led to the multiplication of altars. The altar became the sacred place under which the relics of a saint or martyr were buried, where God's presence and power were believed to secure miracles, healings and other blessings, and to which crowds of pilgrims flocked.

During the Middle Ages altars became more and more ornate and to emphasize their sacredness a baldacchino canopy was built or iconostasis screen erected, for it was on the altar that the most holy sacrifice of the mass was offered and where Christ was made present in the eucharistic elements. The eucharist had become a sacrifice through which one secured God's favour and the number of masses multiplied to ensure an abundance of saving grace.

It is astonishing to discover, however, that by the beginning of the fifth century the practice of receiving communion frequently had declined rapidly in both east and west. There appears to be several reasons for this astounding change in the habits of the laity:

1 The laxity that invaded the Church when persecution was replaced by imperial patronage.
2 The increasing separation of clergy and laity, which suggested that the reception of the eucharist was mainly a clerical duty.
3 The growing demand for temporary sexual abstinence as a prerequisite for communion.
4 The stress on the holy and terrifying character of the consecrated elements, which we have seen first appearing with Cyril of Jerusalem.

It also became no longer necessary for the laity (on the infrequent occasions they did communicate) to receive the cup, with the associated dangers of spilling Christ's blood.

A sense of fear and awe surrounding the eucharist began to dominate popular piety and looking replaced eating and drinking. 'As part of this change, healings increasingly occurred in response to the Eucharistic elements.'[3] It has been said of St Augustine of Hippo (354–430) that 'during one Mass he saw seventy-three people cured instantly of serious illness'.[4] Furthermore, 'as interest in the healing power of the Eucharistic elements increased in the West, celebrants advertised this power through linkages with Mary, at the same time enlisting her to glorify the Eucharist'.[5]

From the beginning of the thirteenth century priests began to raise the newly consecrated bread above their heads, so that the people might see and adore. The sudden appearance of the white circle of the communion host gripped their imagination. Gradually the whole mass came to centre upon the elevation which became the heart of late medieval religion. Couratin describes it thus: 'Bells were rung to attract the attention to the great moment. Torches were held that the people might better see the host. Incense was offered, but care was to be taken that the smoke did not obscure the view'.[6]

Sometimes the people would shout for the priest to lift the host higher so that they could see better. People even started lawsuits in order to ensure a favourable view. The host became the sole object of eucharistic devotion. People ran from church to church to see this moment as many times as they could, often rushing in just beforehand and leaving as hurriedly as they had come. Gazing upon the eucharist at the moment of consecration was thought to produce a salvific effect and rich rewards could be expected from such a practice. Hence the phrase at the elevation of the host – 'the gaze that saves'. Adoration had replaced reception. Crichton, in his book *A Short History of the Mass*, comments: 'There were those who believed that if they attended Mass, or even simply saw the host, they could not grow old that day, that they would not fall ill, that in fact a whole range of natural benefits would accrue to them.'[7]

The establishment of the Feast of Corpus Christi in 1264 became the high point of devotion to the blessed sacrament. Out of this feast came the processions of the blessed sacrament from the fourteenth century and the practice of reserving the sacrament in a prominent place for devotional purposes and communicating the sick. 'As elaborate processions developed to carry the Eucharist to the sick, people congregated along the way for healing and other blessings.'[8] During Corpus Christi processions

> clergy led the Eucharist parade through the streets, accompanied by musical instruments, wagon tableaus, and, of course, expectations of healing. Historian Miri Rubin recounted, 'The host was so powerful that it could even cure by proxy; a woman was cured by an abbot who had touched the host earlier in the day' and 'not through any meritorious act.' Many feared misuse of the Eucharist as a cause of sickness, misfortune and death. Priests took elaborate precautions against dropping or spilling the elements and even worried that magicians might get hold of them.[9]

About 40 supposed eucharistic miracles were also reported to have taken place during the Middle Ages.[10] For example, the famed miracle of Bolsena (*c.* 1263), featured in Raphael's painting that hangs in the Vatican, shows a priest who had doubted the truth of the doctrine of transubstantiation being won over to belief when he sees drops of blood falling from the host.

By now the eucharist had become the subject not just of devotion but also of intellectual speculation. In 1215, the Fourth Lateran Council spoke of the transubstantiation of the bread into the body of Christ and the wine into the blood of Christ to describe the change in the elements. Thomas

Aquinas (1225–74) expressed this change in Aristotelian philosophical categories whereby the 'accidents' of bread and wine (what is perceptible to the senses) remain unchanged, but the 'substance' (the essential inner reality) is miraculously transformed into the body and blood of Christ. These philosophical nuances were, however, far too sophisticated for the average unlettered person to understand.

Abuses of the eucharist became central to the Reformation debate in the sixteenth century. Included in these were the receiving of communion being supplanted by the elevation and adoration of the consecrated elements and the withholding of the cup from the laity, if they ever did receive communion. During the Middle Ages the one unique, historical sacrifice of Christ at the cross was repeated every time mass was said. Luther attacked both the doctrines of transubstantiation and the sacrifice of the mass. Christ was present to be sure and all the benefits of this sacrifice were available to the believer, but Christ himself was not sacrificed, for there could be no repetition of the once-for-all atoning sacrifice of Christ.

Luther also 'completely rejected the idea that healing, or any other blessing from God, might be obtained by means of penance, prayers, saints, or any power inherent in the elements of the Eucharist'.[11] Indeed Luther, Calvin and other Protestant reformers played down the significance of Jesus' healings and other miracles, arguing that they had largely ceased at the end of the apostolic era.

Luther's doctrine of Christ's presence in the sacrament became known as consubstantiation. By this he seems to mean that the bread and wine contain Christ's body and blood rather than actually becoming different substances. The bread and wine are not changed into the body and blood of Christ, but rather the communicant receives the body and blood of Christ with the bread and wine. The consecrated elements, therefore, are both Christ's body and blood and bread and wine. For Zwingli, one of the most extreme of the Protestant reformers whom Luther opposed, the eucharist virtually ceased to be a sacrament at all. It conveyed no grace, but was merely a memorial of Christ's death, celebrated in obedience to his command.

Calvin sought a middle way between Luther and Zwingli, but nevertheless held that Christ is truly present in the eucharist and we feed on him. He said that in the Lord's supper Christ is 'present'. He was reluctant to define how and where Christ is present, preferring instead to say, 'I would rather experience it than understand it.' Another reformer, Martin Bucer, described communion as the means 'by which the sick may be abundantly strengthened in health'. In England Cranmer's eucharistic doctrine is expressed in his 1549 and 1552 prayer books and thereafter in the Church of England 1662 Book of Common Prayer. Cranmer was a receptionist and as such was concerned that communicants should exercise faith, for it was in the act of communion itself, not in the elements, that Christ was present. During the Catholic Counter-Reformation the Council of Trent (1545–63) sought to curb abuses highlighted by the Protestant Reformation, particularly with regard to the eucharist, but without abandoning transubstantiation or the sacrificial character of the mass.

We have fleetingly glimpsed the Reformation scene for, as we shall see later, belief in the real presence of Christ in the sacrament is fundamental to any expectation of its healing power. Queen Elizabeth I, a sensible woman, is said to have dismissed half a century of anguished debate in one brilliant quatrain:

Christ was the Word that spake it,
He took the bread and brake it,
And what his words did make it,
That I believe and take it.

After the Reformation nothing much changed until recent times. For four centuries theological positions remained polarized between the various confessional communities as expressed in four main permanent groups of western eucharistic liturgies – Roman, Lutheran, Calvinist and Anglican. As we have seen, the healing ministry of the Church became downplayed in the Reformation Churches, and in the Roman Church even the sacrament of the anointing of the sick (unction) had become extreme unction as preparation for death. Only with developments such as the shrine at Lourdes was a healing focus maintained.

We noted earlier that all this was to change in the twentieth century, the beginning of which witnessed the birth of the pentecostal movement with its emphasis on gifts of healing and other supernatural phenomena. The birth of the liturgical movement in the west also brought about renewal of the liturgy, leading up to the Second Vatican Council, together with growing ecumenical convergence and rapprochement and a renewed understanding of the eucharist as a healing sacrament.

## Modern liturgies

Recent years have seen extraordinary developments in our understanding of the eucharist. Since the 1960s in western Christianity, eucharistic liturgies of remarkably similar shape have been produced within the various confessional communities, reflecting a considerable degree of theological convergence.

This ecumenical rapprochement can be seen particularly in two documents – the *Agreed Statement of the Anglican–Roman Catholic International Commission* (ARCIC) on the eucharist in 1971, and the *Baptism, Eucharist and Ministry* (BEM) document adopted by the Faith and Order Commission of the World Council of Churches in 1982, in which over 100 theologians, from virtually all the major Church traditions, were involved in producing its convergence texts. In producing its Agreed Statement, ARCIC claimed to 'have reached agreement on essential points of eucharistic doctrine'. Examples of these agreements and consensus reached can be seen, for instance, in the following statements on eucharistic presence:

1 'The elements are not mere signs; Christ's body and blood become really present and are really given.' (ARCIC Eucharistic Doctrine, statement 9)

2 'Through this prayer of thanksgiving, a word of faith addressed to the Father, the bread and wine become the body and blood of Christ by the action of the Holy Spirit, so that in communion we eat the flesh of Christ and drink his blood.' (ARCIC Eucharistic Doctrine, statement 10)

3 'Before the eucharistic prayer, to the question: "What is that?", the believer answers: "It is bread." After the eucharistic prayer, to the same question he answers: "It is truly the body of Christ, the Bread of Life." ' (ARCIC Eucharistic Doctrine, elucidation 6)

4 'The eucharistic meal is the sacrament of the body and blood of Christ, the sacrament of his real presence.' (BEM Eucharist 13)[12]

On 'eucharistic presence' some traditions place the emphasis on Christ's presence in the consecrated elements, while others emphasize his presence in the believer's heart through faith as a result of the act of communion itself. Both these positions need to be held together.

On 'eucharistic sacrifice', we are now seeing a deeper appreciation of metaphorical language which helps us hold together the tension between Christ's once-for-all sacrifice on the cross and the eucharist as a true sacrifice in a sacramental sense.[13] There has been a redefinition of sacrifice in terms of re-presentation rather than repetition. What is really being offered to God at each eucharist is a sacramental re-presentation of the once-for-all historical sacrifice of Christ, making these past saving acts of Christ effective again in the present to the believing community.

It is widely accepted today that the Reformers' vehement rejection of the medieval Roman doctrines of *presence* and *sacrifice* had been occasioned by the distorted Catholic teaching and practical abuses at that time. An overreaction inevitably led them to 'throw out the baby with the bath water'. As can be seen in the ARCIC and BEM texts, however, a considerable degree of theological convergence has been reached on the eucharist in our own day.

Matters of eucharistic sacrifice and presence have merited extended consideration, given their important bearing on the eucharist as a healing sacrament. Indeed, the real and sacrificial presence of Christ in this sacrament is fundamental to its effectiveness as a sacrament of healing. We now look at a selection of liturgical texts to be found in modern Roman Catholic and Anglican eucharistic liturgies that relate to healing, examining first the Roman texts.

Prayer for healing in one form or another is an important theme in every Roman mass. The private prayers of preparation before mass include the prayers of St Thomas Aquinas and St Ambrose, both of which look for healing (extracts of which can be found on pages 111–13).

There are a number of prayers over the gifts of bread and wine at the offertory that refer directly to health and healing, for example:

All powerful God, may the healing power of this sacrifice free us from sin and help us to approach you with pure hearts. (Friday, 4th week of Lent)

Lord, you have given us these gifts to honour your name. Bless them, and let them become a source of health and strength. (Wednesday, 5th week of Lent)

Lord God, in this bread and wine you give us food for body and spirit. May the eucharist renew our strength and bring us health of mind and body. (Week XI)

Lord, we bring you these gifts to become the health-giving body and blood of your Son. In his name heal the ills which afflict us and restore to us the joy of life renewed. (Anointing within Mass)

In one of the personal liturgical prayers, as part of the priest's private preparation before receiving communion, these words are quietly said:

> Lord Jesus Christ, with faith in your love and mercy I eat your body and drink your blood. Let it not bring me condemnation, but health in mind and body.

One of the most important healing texts in the Roman mass (and also in Anglican rites) is the prayer said in response to the invitation to communion in which we are, in some way, replicating the healing faith of the centurion in Matthew 8.8:

> Lord, I am not worthy to receive you, but only say the word and I shall be healed.

A number of the prayers after communion ask for healing, for example:

> Lord, through this sacrament may we rejoice in your healing power and experience your saving love in mind and body. (Monday, 1st week of Lent)

> Lord, may the mysteries we receive heal us, remove sin from our hearts and make us grow strong under your constant protection. (Wednesday, 5th week of Lent)

> Lord, may this eucharist increase within us the healing power of your love. May it guide and direct our efforts to please you in all things. (Week XXI)

> Lord our God, renew us by these mysteries. May they heal us now and bring us eternal salvation. (Thursday, 1st week of Lent)

In the Church of England *Common Worship* eucharistic rites there are a number of references to healing; for example in *Pastoral Services* (p. 28), the introductory prayer of penitence (Kyrie eleison) for the laying on of hands with prayer and anointing at a celebration of holy communion:

Lord Jesus, you healed the sick:
Lord, have mercy.
Lord Jesus, you forgave sinners:
Christ, have mercy.
Lord Jesus, you give yourself to heal us and bring us strength:
Lord, have mercy.

In *Common Worship: Services and Prayers for the Church of England*, a Eucharistic Prayer (Order One, Prayer F) contains the intercession:

Look with favour on your people and in your mercy hear the cry of our hearts. Bless the earth, heal the sick, let the oppressed go free and fill your Church with power from on high.

A proper preface in the eucharistic prayer for use in particular sickness, especially when the sick have been anointed, reads:

And now we give you thanks
because you provide medicine to heal our sickness,
and the leaves of the tree of life
for the healing of the nations,
anointing us with your healing power
so that we may be the first fruits of your new creation.

A post-communion prayer states:

God of all mercy, in this Eucharist you have set aside our sins and given us your healing: grant that we who are made whole in Christ may bring that healing to this broken world. (Trinity 12)

There are several other references to healing in both Roman and Anglican eucharistic liturgies.

## Administration of the sacrament

We need not dwell long on this, for we are not looking at how each confessional community administers holy communion generally as part of its worship, but only as it relates specifically to healing. Suffice to say that each confessional community has its own way of distributing the sacrament.

Roman Catholics and Anglicans generally use a chalice and wafer breads, although Catholics until recently (and still even now in many churches) administered in one kind only: the eucharistic bread. Given their greater and more frequent number of communicants this has no doubt been for practical and pastoral reasons, and the doctrine of concomitance states that Christ's body and blood is sacramentally present under each of the species of bread and wine. However, 'the sign of Communion is more complete when given under both kinds'.[14]

In the main, Methodists and Baptists are still wedded to small individual cups to administer the wine, even though the ideal symbol is the sharing of the one cup. However, unlike all Roman Catholic and most Anglican churches they generally partake of the one loaf, rather than individual wafers, which is a fuller sign of the unity of the Church, following St Paul: 'We who are many are one body, for we all partake of the one bread' (1 Corinthians 10.17). Orthodox churches tend to administer the sacrament by intinction, whereby the bread is soaked in the wine and administered on a spoon.

It is the norm in Roman Catholic churches for the sacrament to be celebrated not only on Sundays but daily throughout the week, sometimes several times a day in very large churches in England, and the first mass of Sunday is often on a Saturday evening. It is an obligation on Roman Catholics to attend mass each Sunday and on other holy days of obligation (e.g. Ascension Day). Many Anglican churches have a single mid-week celebration of the eucharist, though in the Catholic wing of the Church of England this can be almost a daily celebration, and in one well-known Anglo-Catholic church in central London takes place three times daily. Anglican churches tend to permit all baptized or confirmed members of other churches to receive communion, but Roman Catholics stipulate that, other than in special circumstances, only Catholics can receive the sacrament in their churches, though flexibility has been exercised by some priests on this without authority.[15]

All churches encourage those not able to receive communion to receive a blessing. I recall an amusing incident when our son was a little boy. We were on holiday and visiting a small village church one Sunday. During the service our son wanted to go to the toilet, and as there wasn't one in the church my wife took him outside in the churchyard and then they returned to their seats. At the distribution of communion my wife and son went to the altar rail, my wife to receive communion and my son a blessing. The priest laid his hand on our son's head, and using a biblical quotation said: 'The Lord bless thy going out and thy coming in.' With that my son looked at my wife rather embarrassed and exclaimed, 'Mum, he saw me go out and have a piddle!' On another occasion I was administering communion, and at the end of the service a little boy said to his grandmother, 'I don't like that man in church!' 'Why not?' his grandmother asked. 'Well, he put his hand on my head and said sumfink, but he didn't give *me* a pill and a drink.' He was given a Polo at the end of the service the following week to keep him quiet.

*The Catechism of the Catholic Church* states: 'The Lord addresses an invitation to us, urging us to receive him in the sacrament of the Eucharist. "Truly I say to you, unless you eat the flesh of the Son of Man and drink his blood, you have no life in you" (John 6.53). To respond to this invitation we must *prepare ourselves* for so great and so holy a moment.'[16] It quotes 1 Corinthians 11.27–29, where St Paul urges us to examine our conscience before receiving the sacrament. The Catechism states: 'Anyone conscious of a grave sin must receive the sacrament of Reconciliation before coming to communion',[17] and goes on to say: 'Daily conversion and penance find their source and nourishment in the Eucharist, for in it is made present the sacrifice of Christ which has reconciled us with God. Through the Eucharist those who live from the life of Christ are fed and strengthened. It is a remedy to free us from our daily faults and to preserve us from mortal sins.'[18]

In all Roman Catholic churches and many Anglican ones the sacrament is reserved for administering to the sick at home or in hospital, as well as for devotional purposes. This, of course, presupposes belief that Christ's presence in the consecrated elements continues after the celebration of the eucharist from which it was reserved, upon which not all Protestant churches agree. It was sometimes said that it took more faith to make Roman Catholic school children believe that communion wafers are bread than it did to make them believe that the bread becomes Christ's body.

We have seen in the Church of England *Common Worship: Pastoral Services* rites of 'Wholeness and Healing' that provision is made for the distribution of holy communion at home or in hospital to the sick and housebound. Likewise, in the Roman Catholic Church there are two rites for communion of the sick, one for ordinary circumstances (e.g. in the home) and one for communion in a hospital or institution. Priests with pastoral responsibilities are urged that the sick and aged 'are given every opportunity to receive the eucharist frequently, even daily' and that 'to provide frequent communion for the sick, it may be necessary to ensure that the community has a sufficient number of ministers of communion'.[19] There are also rites provided for anointing of the sick within mass and, of course, for the celebration of the eucharist as viaticum, food for the passage through death to eternal life, which is the sacrament proper to the dying.

Before concluding consideration of the administration of the sacrament it should be noted how important prayer for healing is within this context. MacNutt comments:

> I know of at least half a dozen healings that have taken place during the Mass without any prayers being said other than those in the liturgical form; and I think I can

say I have seen hundreds of healings take place when I have added special prayers for healing after Communion, or immediately after Mass is over. As a time for healing I would prefer praying with the community during the Mass than at any other time I know of – at that time when Jesus Christ is most especially among us.[20]

I came across a sermon recently that featured a comparison between two paintings of the Last Supper. One is by a Flemish artist of the sixteenth century, and hangs in Belvoir Castle. As in the famous picture of 'The Last Supper' by Leonardo da Vinci, painted some 50 years earlier, the 12 disciples sit with Jesus around a long table as he blesses the bread and wine. In da Vinci's picture the disciples are attentive and reverent, immersed in the significance of the moment and their devotion to their Lord. The painting you see at Belvoir shows something quite different. In the centre a calm and dignified Jesus blesses the food placed upon the table, but all around him is chaos and disarray. Some of the disciples are engaged in animated private conversations with their neighbours; others are looking bored and have turned away to stare vacantly into space; one has much too large a pitcher of wine, and to cap it all a couple of dogs are fighting under the table. It is a picture of confusion that makes one smile. But it has a serious point. For the gift of bread and wine is given not just into the reverence and serenity of a setting such as we enjoy in a church, but into the disorder and muddle of our everyday lives.

## The importance of the eucharist

A young priest colleague was telling me of an occasion during a post-ordination training session with other young priests, most from an evangelical background. They were asked what evangelistic efforts they were involved with in their churches. When his time came to speak, he said: 'I celebrate the eucharist.'

Thinking it was a joke, there was much chuckling, but my colleague was making a serious point. The eucharist is an evangelistic tool like no other, for St Paul said: 'As often as you eat this bread and drink this cup, you *proclaim* the Lord's death until he comes' (1 Corinthians 11.26).

The eucharist is far more than a liturgy or the administration of a ritual or sacrament. Its crucial importance is in the life it imparts, the life of God. In a talk given to priests at a healing seminar the Revd Tommy Tyson, a Methodist evangelist, stated:

> You stand before the Holy Table and you break that wafer. You say these words 'This is my body', and you say, 'Take and eat.' Do you mean that I can eat the body of Jesus without appropriating health? What could be a greater healing ministry than the sacraments? 'This is my blood which is shed for you.' Does it just go into my digestive tract and that's the end of it? Isn't there some way for the average layman to appropriate that healing grace which goes through his entire body, mind and spirit? Did God simply give you a liturgy, or did he give you a way of bringing people life?[21]

Bob Webber, President of the Institute for Worship Studies in Chicago, wrote in *Planning Blended Worship*:

> An intense encounter with God's supernatural presence is supposed to take place in the receiving of bread and wine, but this experience has been terribly damaged by modern thinking. Enlightenment rationalism persuaded both liberals and conservatives that the bread and wine were empty symbols, mere memorials to trigger the mind towards the cross and the idea of sacrificial love. Consequently, there has been no divine encounter during the taking of the bread and wine; it has become all human recall, human intent, human sentiment. Now, however, in the

current post-enlightenment renewal of the supernatural, there is a new appreciation of the mystery of Christ's saving and healing presence in communion.[22]

In a lecture entitled 'What is Christianity?' given at the International Islamic University in Islamabad, Pakistan (27 November 2005), the Archbishop of Canterbury, Rowan Williams said: 'When they (Christians) bless bread and wine in his name, the sharing of this food and drink will be an occasion for God's new life to enter into them afresh. Just as Jesus' human flesh and blood is the place where God's power and Spirit are at work, so in this bread and wine, blessed in his memory, the same power and Spirit are active.'

The following statements come from *A Time to Heal*, a major report on the healing ministry for the House of Bishops of the General Synod of the Church of England:

1  The Eucharist is essentially a service of healing even though many lay people do not appreciate it as such. (p. 37)
2  One effect of the liturgical revision in recent years has been to reveal more clearly the Eucharist as the healing service *par excellence*. (p. 269)
3  All Christian churches celebrate the Eucharist, although not all of those who attend and receive Holy Communion realize that this celebration is the most common form of 'healing service' in its widest and truest sense. (p. 64)
4  The Eucharist is the highest liturgical celebration of thanksgiving for healing. (p. 324)

An earlier Church of England report on the Church's Ministry of Healing commented: 'The objectivity of the Church's worship in Holy Communion is . . . a salutary corrective to the subjective and emotional tone which can easily become dominant in healing services.'[23] Dr Martin Israel, a priest and medical doctor, whose writings have been an inspiration to many, said in his book *Healing as Sacrament* that 'the Eucharist is the principal healing sacrament of the Church'.[24]

*The Catechism of the Catholic Church* states that the Church 'believes in the life-giving presence of Christ, the physician of souls and bodies. This presence is particularly active through the sacraments, and in an altogether special way through the Eucharist, the bread that gives eternal life and that St Paul suggests is connected with bodily health'[25] (see John 6.54; 1 Corinthians 11.30). Indeed 'the Eucharist is the source and summit of the Christian life',[26] 'toward which the activity of the Church is directed; it is also the fount from which all her power flows'.[27]

John Hampsch, in his book *The Healing Power of the Eucharist*, points out that 'the Eucharist is a healing sacrament because, in receiving this sacrament, we are touching Jesus, the Healer himself, and he is touching us'.[28] Like the woman who, in faith, touched the fringe of Jesus' clothes, power goes out from him to heal (Luke 8.43–48). Hampsch states: 'Regrettably, many people do not even think of healing as available through the Eucharist or know how Communion can be a source of healing for them.'[29] He comments on John 6.56, 'Those who eat my flesh and drink my blood abide in me, and I in them': 'Jesus abides in us, but we do not really abide in him as we should. By not responding to the transforming power available in the Eucharist, we truncate the healing power that we would otherwise receive; we deprive ourselves of God's power and we obtund God's work within us.'[30]

Hampsch draws attention to ways in which we can hinder the working of God's grace in the eucharist according to our disposition. A lack of faith, love, devotion and hunger for the bread of life, or the presence of sin, can hinder to some extent the flow of grace, whereas a right disposition involving expectant faith taps the full power of this sacrament. The amount of grace we receive in the sacrament, therefore, is in accordance with our disposition. The same, he says, is true over the amount of healing we receive. 'Everyone will receive a little healing in some way, but some will receive truly astonishing healings.'[31]

The ultimate goal of the eucharist is not the transformation of the elements of bread and wine but rather the transformation of those who receive those transformed elements. Cardinal Cormac Murphy-O'Connor wrote in his white paper to the Roman Catholic Diocese of Westminster (February 2006) entitled 'Communion and Mission: Pastoral Priorities for the Diocese of Westminster': 'Our prayer must be rooted in a deeper understanding and appreciation of the Holy Eucharist.' He said, 'I believe that deepening our understanding of this gift will be a major priority in the years ahead.'

## *Sister Briege McKenna*

This section is concerned with the worldwide healing ministry of the Roman Catholic nun Sister Briege McKenna, who describes in her book *Miracles Do Happen* some remarkable healings that have taken place as a result of the power of the eucharist to heal. In view of the astounding claims made in the book, I asked a Jesuit priest, a university lecturer who taught me liturgy, for his opinion about her. He felt that she had a fertile imagination, but knew that if she was due to speak publicly somewhere many priests would express an interest in hearing her. Let me recount some of these stories from her book.

At one outdoor mass in a mountainous Latin American country a little boy was brought who was suffering from very severe burns and sores on his body. He was left to sit under a table. McKenna was overwhelmed at the participation of the people in the celebration as the priest, who had a deep personal faith in Jesus and an excitement about the mass, made it come alive for these very poor people. At the consecration she saw that people were prostrate on the ground:

> They lifted up their eyes to adore the Lord. The look on their faces made me think, 'They really believe that this is Jesus.' Then when I looked at the sacred Host, in my own

imagination, I got the most beautiful image of Jesus with his two hands out. He was smiling with great love and compassion. He was embracing these poor people and saying, 'Come to me, all who are weary, and I will give you life and faith.'

This was the moment that I realized in the depths of my heart, 'Dear Jesus, this is really you. It may look like bread and a cup, but only you could think of such a creative way to make yourself present to your people.'

After the mass, I went around to see how the little boy was. He had been placed under the table which served as the altar. But he wasn't there. I said to the woman who had brought him to the mass, 'Where is he?' She said, pointing to a group of children playing nearby, 'There he is.' I looked at the child and he was fine. There wasn't a thing wrong with his little body. I said aloud, but more to myself, 'What happened to him?' The old woman looked at me and said, 'What do you mean, "What happened?". Didn't Jesus come?'[32]

McKenna goes on:

That same day, at the beginning of mass, I also saw a little boy who had a terrible facial deformity. At the end of the mass, his mother came running up to me with her child in her arms. She said 'Sister, look at my little boy.' The boy's face was healed. I was the one who was very surprised.[33]

McKenna said that she left that mountain with a completely new understanding of the eucharist. She was unable to sleep that night and felt that God was telling her to point people to him in the eucharist, to make him known to people in the eucharist, rather than them making false gods out of people in healing ministries.

Another story is of a young priest who had cancer of the vocal cords and was soon to have his voice box removed. He telephoned McKenna, who told him, 'Every day at mass, when you touch the sacred host and eat it you are meeting Jesus, like the woman who touched the hem of Jesus' garment and was healed, only you are actually receiving him into your body.' She said to him: 'Do you realize that Jesus is actually going down your throat? There is no better one to go to than Jesus. You ask Jesus to heal you.'[34] Some will have reservations about this localized way of describing Christ's presence in the eucharist.

It turned out that, unknown to McKenna at the time, this young priest had stopped celebrating mass except on Sundays and had become very flippant about it. She heard him crying on the phone saying, 'Oh, Sister, thank you. Thank you.' Three weeks later he went for surgery, but didn't require it, for the doctors discovered the cancer was gone and his vocal cords were healed as if brand new. This experience transformed this priest's life, for as well as being healed he became a eucharist-centred priest.

McKenna also tells of a woman with inoperable stomach cancer who came with expectant faith that Jesus would heal her in the eucharist. As she swallowed the host she felt something burning her throat and down into her stomach. The growth was healed. McKenna concludes: 'If you come to mass with the right attitude, your life will change. Our churches are often packed with people who come and leave the same way. You ask yourself, "Is it Jesus? Did he change? Is he not fulfilling his promises?" Or could it be that I do not have the expectant faith to allow him to touch my life and answer my needs?'[35]

McKenna writes of a practice that Fr Kevin Scanlon and she adopted in the Far East. In a stadium filled with over 20,000 people Fr Scanlon walked down the aisles carrying a monstrance. Having been taught about Jesus being truly present in the eucharist, people were encouraged to raise their hands towards the monstrance containing the sacred host and to ask Jesus to bless them and heal them. She stressed the need to focus attention and faith on the Lord, for there is always a danger of people looking to a minister instead of the Lord.

She described an experience of this practice in Hawaii. Fr Scanlon was processing the blessed sacrament along the aisles. A Mormon girl who had deformed hands had hoped to be prayed for, but as people were not being prayed for individually, everyone was encouraged to focus on Jesus in the blessed sacrament. Fr Scanlon held up the monstrance and blessed the people. Looking at the host this girl 'felt something come from it and go through her body. As she walked out of the church, she nudged her Catholic friend and said "Look". She held out her hands and they were healed.'[36]

On a CD recording of an address entitled 'Understanding the Eucharist' given at a retreat for nuns in Ireland during 'The Year of the Eucharist' (October 2004–October 2005), Sister McKenna provides further details of some of the events recorded in her book *Miracles Do Happen*. At the outdoor mass recounted above, she tells of the healing of a one-year-old boy of Down's syndrome. She also describes the power of the intimacy with Jesus in the eucharist by referring to events that happened in Sydney and in Florida. We begin with the incident in Sydney.

McKenna was approached by a woman named Karen, aged about 35, who had been diagnosed with cancer of the liver and stomach and was scared of dying. She had six children, the youngest of which was two years old. This woman had heard of Briege McKenna's ministry and asked her to heal her. McKenna stated:

I told this woman that at 4 p.m. in the church over there, there's going to be a mass. Jesus is going to be present and you can personally meet the Jesus of the Bible. He's going to be in that church and he can heal you. I don't know whether you're going to get physically healed, but I can guarantee you that you will not be in the mess you are in now. When you go up to receive holy communion and say, 'Lord I am not worthy to receive you but only say the word and I shall be healed' – that is Jesus and he longs to come to us. When you receive holy communion, people may say that it may not be God's will for us to be healed. Take your chance and let him make up his own mind. Don't be afraid to ask. At the end of that day at about 9.30 p.m. she came running up to me. She was aglow. She said, 'Sister Briege. I don't know whether I'm healed', but she said, 'Today was the first day I ever celebrated mass' (she'd been going to mass since she was a child). Up until that day she fulfilled an obligation. She was so excited that she was going to meet Jesus, but she'd been meeting Jesus all her life, but she didn't recognize him, she said.

When she went up there she brought all her children with her including the baby and the whole time she kept thinking, 'O God, I'm going to meet you personally, the same as the woman who touched your garment.' She said, 'I was so excited at the awareness that this was Jesus, I had a whole list of things about my husband and children and so on, that when the priest said, "The body of Christ", I said, "O Jesus, give me everything!" ' And the priest just looked at her and probably thought, 'What a nutcase this is.' She said, 'I shall never forget, Sister, the peace. I had been so thirsty up until then. I was doing God a favour, but this time it was the reverse. My soul was thirsting for the living God and he quenched my thirst.' She said, 'It was like something warm going over ice. Everything melted, including the fear of death.' She said, 'I can't explain it, but I don't know whether I want to live or die now. I don't know what to pray for I'm so happy.' She was radiant. Three days later she went back to the hospital and the newspaper carried her story. She was completely healed of cancer. – It happens all the time.

In her retreat address McKenna also told the story of a 23-year-old student from the University of Florida who had cancer. Her father was a doctor and in his surgery she had found, among a pile of magazines, a copy of McKenna's book *Miracles Do Happen*. She and her family were lapsed Catholics. She read the book, then telephoned every convent she could find to trace Briege McKenna. When she eventually found her they met and went into the chapel. They knelt and prayed in front of the blessed sacrament in the tabernacle. Soon after, Briege McKenna left the convent to travel, but when she returned a couple of months later one of the sisters told her about a man who had been kneeling in front of a statue outside the convent. He was the girl's father and he said that his daughter had gone to confession as a lapsed Catholic, and then started going to mass daily. The next time she went to her doctor she was perfect. Not only that, but her whole family came back to the faith and her father was kneeling to give thanks.

These are some of the remarkable healings through the sacrament of the eucharist that are purported to have taken place in the ongoing worldwide ministry of Sister Briege McKenna. Sceptical doctors and others, however, will no doubt point out that it can take years of scans, tests and subsequent good health to prove that someone has been permanently cured of cancer, for example.

## The eucharist and sin

*The Catechism of the Catholic Church* states:

> Holy Communion separates us from sin. The body of Christ we receive in Holy Communion is 'given up for us', and the blood we drink 'shed for the many for the forgiveness of sins'. For this reason the Eucharist cannot unite us to Christ without at the same time cleansing us from past sins and preserving us from future sins: For as often as we eat this bread and drink this cup, we proclaim the death of the Lord. If we proclaim the Lord's death,

we proclaim the forgiveness of sins. If, as often as his blood is poured out, it is poured for the forgiveness of sins, I should always receive it, so that it may always forgive my sins. Because I always sin, I should always have a remedy.[37]

The Catechism goes on to say: 'As bodily nourishment restores lost strength, so the Eucharist strengthens our charity, which tends to be weakened in daily life; and this living charity *wipes away venial sins*.'[38] 'By the same charity that it enkindles in us, the Eucharist *preserves us from future mortal sins*.'[39] In order for this preservation to be effective, however, our wills need to be aligned with the divine will to ensure that there is an unimpeded channel through which the transference of divine grace can flow.

In the 1662 Church of England Book of Common Prayer there is a general warning about the seriousness of holy communion and the need to examine our consciences before partaking of it. An exhortation is given that we are in great danger if we receive the sacrament unworthily, for 'we eat and drink our own damnation, not considering the Lord's Body; we kindle God's wrath against us; we provoke him to plague us with divers diseases, and sundry kinds of death. Judge therefore yourselves, brethren, that ye be not judged of the Lord; repent you truly for your sins past.'

Two prayers of preparation in the Roman Weekday and Sunday Missals focus on sin, contrition, penitence, forgiveness and healing. Here are some extracts.

*Prayer of St Ambrose*

Lord Jesus Christ,
I approach your banquet table in fear and trembling, for
    I am a sinner,
and dare not rely on my own worth, but only on your
    goodness and mercy.

111

I am defiled by many sins in body and soul, and by my
  unguarded thoughts and words.
Gracious God of majesty and awe, I seek your protection,
  I look for your healing.
Poor troubled sinner that I am, I appeal to you, the
  fountain of all mercy . . .
I repent my sins, and I long to put right what I have
  done.
Merciful Father, take away all my offences and sins;
purify me in body and soul, and make me worthy to
  taste the holy of holies.
May your body and blood which I intend to receive,
  although I am unworthy,
be for me the remission of my sins, the washing away of
  my guilt,
the end of my evil thoughts, and the rebirth of my
  better instincts.
May it incite me to do the works pleasing to you and
  profitable to my health in body and soul and be a
  firm defence against the wiles of my enemies. Amen.

*Prayer of St Thomas Aquinas*

Almighty and everlasting God,
I draw near to the sacrament of your only-begotten
  Son, our Lord Jesus Christ.
I who am sick approach the physician of life. I who am
  unclean come to the fountain of mercy; blind, to the
  light of eternal brightness;
poor and needy, to the Lord of heaven and earth.
Therefore, I implore you, in your boundless mercy, to
  heal my sickness, cleanse my defilement, enlighten
  my blindness, enrich my poverty, and clothe my
  nakedness.
Then shall I dare to receive the bread of angels, the King
  of kings and Lord of lords,

with reverence and humility, contrition and love, purity
   and faith,
with the purpose and intention necessary for the good
   of my soul.
Grant, I beseech you, that I may receive not only the
   Body and Blood of the Lord, but also the grace and
   power of the sacrament . . .
Most loving Father, grant that I may one day see face to
   face your beloved Son,
whom I now intend to receive under the veil of the
   sacrament,
and who with you and the Holy Spirit,
lives and reigns for ever, one God, world without end.
   Amen.

I once heard an influential evangelical preacher, David Pawson, one-time minister of a large Baptist church in Guildford, Surrey, preach on 1 Corinthians 10 and 11 about the presence of Christ in the eucharistic bread and wine and about the power of these elements to bring judgement, and therefore conversely blessing and healing. If I can remember accurately from my notes what he said, he referred to the bread and wine being more than mere symbols, because we eat and drink these symbols; we make them disappear. If they were just here to remind us of the cross, then we need do nothing more than keep bread and wine on the communion table to look at during the service. We could just sit and watch bread being broken and wine poured out; that's all we need to see. But they don't stay on the table, they disappear; we eat and drink them. What is the point, he asked, of eating and drinking if they are simply mementoes? What a strange thing to do with a memento. Why will we eat it? Why will we drink it? Because in so doing we are nourishing our souls and bodies on Christ, whom we have contacted in the real way that he promised to us. It is the communion of his body.

Pawson stated that Jesus Christ is in the highest heaven now even though his Spirit is with us. We can pray to him there, but we can have unique contact with him in this sacrament. It is a means of union with him, of contacting him in highest heaven. Therefore, he said, we approach this sacrament reverently and with a deep sense of awe. 'The cup of blessing that we bless, is it not a sharing in the blood of Christ? The bread that we break, is it not a sharing in the body of Christ?' (1 Corinthians 10.16).

Pawson drew attention to 1 Corinthians 11.27–30: 'Whoever, therefore, eats the bread or drinks the cup of the Lord in an unworthy manner will be answerable for the body and blood of the Lord . . . All who eat and drink without discerning the body, eat and drink judgement against themselves. For this reason many of you are weak and ill, and some have died.' Pawson said, 'Now tell me, can mere bread and wine do that to you?' He commented: 'This sacrament can actually do you harm this morning. Physical harm. You could even die as a result of taking it, according to St Paul. Now can symbols do that to you? If the bread and wine were merely symbols of the past they could do no damage. But according to the New Testament, not only can they bring you into communion with a Christ to bless, they can bring you into contact with a Christ to punish, and to eat and drink unworthily is to be open to being physically ill and even dying. That wouldn't be possible if it were merely a memorial. The bread and wine actually puts us through to God and we can have communion with him. And if you come to the holy communion unworthily you are trifling with the body and blood of Christ.' Pawson concluded: 'Holy communion is more special than prayer or preaching, for nowhere in the Bible do you fall sick and even die of prayer and preaching, but you can of this – there's something deeper here.' The corollary of this is that if this eucharistic food can do such damage when received unworthily, how much more will it be medicine and healing if received worthily. If taking it unworthily can bring sickness, then taking it worthily can bring health.

We noted earlier that in the Middle Ages the eucharist was seen as a sacrifice offered to God repeatedly to secure his saving grace and favour, including obtaining forgiveness of sins and other health-related benefits. We have also seen in recent ecumenical discussions a theological redefinition of the sacrifice of the mass in terms of it being a re-presentation of the once-for-all historical sacrifice of Christ on the cross, rather than a repetition, which makes the past saving acts of Christ effective again in the present. Perhaps another way of describing this pastorally could be in terms of *re-application*. Faith in the promises and work of Christ in the Bible constantly has to be applied by the Christian. It is no use believing certain things if we do not apply them, put them into practice and let them take effect in our lives; they might as well remain in the Bible. It is rather like going to the doctor to get a prescription to treat some condition. If we don't then take it along to the pharmacist to obtain the medicine, the prescription is to no avail. It is no good knowing that we have the remedy if we do not then apply it, by putting the ointment on the wound, for instance. It is the same with the wound of sin, to which we can apply and experience God's forgiveness and healing in an objective way in the eucharist, rather than rely on our own subjective feelings of self-worth and acceptance by God.

The frequent *re-application* of the once-for-all sacrifice of Christ in the eucharist ensures that we continually 'obtain remission of our sins and all other benefits of his passion' (Book of Common Prayer) and are 'abundantly strengthened in health' (Martin Bucer), including the strength we need to preserve us from future sins if we have a right disposition. In this way the sacrifice of Christ is not just a memorial of a past event; when applied in the eucharist it becomes effective for our health and spiritual well-being now, for in this sacrament we are receiving Christ whose blood washes away our sins. None of this, of course, negates what has been said about the sacrament of penance/reconciliation, which is particularly important for the confession of major (mortal) sins, and can also be used for the wiping away of venial sins that have accumulated over a period of time and have not been confessed and healed, or wiped away through receiving holy communion.

## Food for the journey

A phrase like 'the journey of life' is one of the central metaphors of our culture. Christians also talk about their faith journey. We are familiar with John Bunyan's *Pilgrim's Progress*. The Christian's spiritual pilgrimage begins as it did for Mary and Joseph with the journey to Bethlehem, where the Christ child was born. Jesus, who would later call himself 'the bread of life', was laid as a newborn infant in a manger, a box designed to hold food for the livestock in the stable.

An editorial in *The Times* on Christmas Eve 2001 reminded us that:

> Bethlehem means 'the house of bread', and so it is that generations of Christians have found their Bethlehem in the broken bread of the Eucharist and have known the heart and strength of Christmas in the worship of the Midnight Mass at which the child in the manger is the bread of life given into our hands to feed us and into our lives to transform us.

At the other end of his life, following his death and resurrection, Jesus is found on the road to Emmaus drawing alongside two disciples who were 'kept from recognizing him'. When they drew near to the village he sat at the table with them, took bread, blessed and broke it, and gave it to them. Then their eyes were opened, and they recognized him; and he vanished from their sight. When the two travellers returned to Jerusalem, they recounted to the eleven and their companions what had happened on the road, 'and how he had been made known to them in the breaking of the bread' (Luke 24.35). Since then, countless followers of Jesus have recognized him in the breaking of the bread in which he has made himself known to them.

Pope John Paul II in his 14th Encyclical in April 2002 on the eucharist commented: 'Whenever the Church celebrates the Eucharist, the faithful can in some way relive the experience of the two disciples on the road to Emmaus: "Their eyes were opened and they recognised him."' The eucharist, the Pope affirmed, 'is the most precious possession which the Church can have in her journey through history'. He went on: 'Each day my faith has been able to recognise in the consecrated bread and wine the divine wayfarer who joined the two disciples on the road to Emmaus and opened their eyes to the light and their hearts to new hope.' He said of the eucharist: 'We can hear in the depths of our hearts, as if they were addressed to us, the same words heard by the Prophet Elijah: "Arise and eat, else the journey will be too great for you."'

I once had the privilege of attending the Corpus Christi mass at Arundel Cathedral, with its magnificent carpet of flowers down the centre aisle of the nave, over which at the end of mass the blessed sacrament was processed on its way to the castle where benediction was given. On that occasion Bishop Cormac Murphy-O'Connor, then Roman Catholic Bishop of Arundel and Brighton (subsequently Cardinal Archbishop of Westminster) was the preacher.

His homily described how as a young boy he and his older brothers used to go to Ireland for their holidays. His father decided one year that Cormac's three brothers should go on a cycling holiday to Ireland. Along their route through the west of England and South Wales, he had postal orders put in post offices in every big town, as you could do in those days. They only ever had enough money and supplies to get them as far as the next post office, there to stock up on provisions and go on to the next place. Their mother was very fearful. She thought constantly of these poor boys and waited to hear from them. Eventually a postcard came through. They had just crossed over on the boat and the postcard said, jokingly, 'All sick. No money.' Bishop Cormac used this story to parallel our journey through life. Every step along the way God has given us in the eucharist sustenance for the journey, sufficient for each next step along the way, until we reach our destination on the other side.

My wife suffers from bronchiectasis, which is a debilitating condition. The base of the lungs is damaged and she is well cared for by her consultants. We continue to pray for healing. I was reading of a woman whose lungs have been seriously sick for years who is the coordinator of a large prayer group. What greatly surprises her doctors is that someone with her lungs can live the very active and fruitful life she does. Those close to her felt that the healing and strengthening power of Jesus in the eucharist was, in her case, a large part of the explanation. It is encouraging to see how Christians on their pilgrim journey are sustained by God, within the context of ongoing medical care.

The final prayer after communion in the Church of England *Common Worship* rites reminds us that our sustenance for the Christian journey is not mere bread and wine but the body and blood of Jesus Christ: 'Almighty God, we thank you for feeding us with the body and blood of your son Jesus Christ . . . Send us out in the power of your Spirit to live and work to your praise and glory.' This food sustains, nourishes, strengthens, empowers and heals us. Then, one day, when the fever of life is over and our work done, this sacrament becomes our sacred food to strengthen us for the passage through death to life eternal. It is viaticum, food for the journey, for the passing over. A *Common Worship* post-communion prayer says: 'God our creator, you feed your children with the true manna, the living bread from heaven: let this holy food sustain us through our earthly pilgrimage until we come to that place where hunger and thirst are no more.'

## *Strength in weakness*

St Paul was one of the most gifted and talented men of his day. He had extraordinary encounters with God. Yet he wrote in 2 Corinthians 12.7–10:

> To keep me from being too elated, a thorn was given me in the flesh, a messenger of Satan to torment me, to keep me from being too elated. Three times I appealed to the Lord about this, that it would leave me, but he said to me, 'My grace is sufficient for you, for my power is made perfect in weakness.' So I will boast all the more gladly of my weaknesses, so that the power of Christ may dwell in me . . . for whenever I am weak, then I am strong.

We do not know what Paul's 'thorn in the flesh' was. Many suggestions have been made, ranging from an eye problem to demonic oppression (for he speaks of his thorn being a 'messenger of Satan' to torment him).

Despite the strong faith of St Paul and others (after all, Paul performed miracles on occasions), not every prayer in the New Testament received a 'yes' answer. Paul's thorn in the flesh wasn't removed. However, his prayer didn't go unanswered. Paul heard God speak, but it wasn't an answer he, or many of us, would welcome. God said, 'My grace is sufficient for you, for my power is made perfect in weakness.' Paul prayed that his thorn in the flesh might be taken from him, but God answered that prayer in the way he answers so many prayers – he didn't take the thing away, but gave Paul strength to bear it. That is how God often works. He doesn't always spare us things, but makes us able to conquer them. This helps us to understand so-called unanswered prayer.

Instead of taking away Paul's difficulty, God gave him grace, the gift of divine power, to bear his thorn in the flesh. We want God to transform our circumstances; but more often God is interested in transforming us. To remove the thorn would have left Paul unchanged and prone to boasting. To have to endure it and yet to be provided with grace to overcome his problem enabled Paul's life continually to be transformed. God's grace is sufficient, because his power comes to full strength when we are weak. It is our inadequacy and insufficiency that opens the door for God's sufficiency to work in our lives, as it did in St Paul's. That truth delivers Christians from the burden of always striving to prove themselves, as though the power in a Christian's life depends on their own resources. Paul's weakness made room in his life for Christ's power to take up residence in him.

St Paul says elsewhere in 2 Corinthians: 'But we have this treasure in clay jars, so that it may be made clear that this extraordinary power belongs to God and does not come from us' (2 Corinthians 4.7). Christians are 'crackpots' – cracked pots. The power of the Christian message is placed in weak containers that crack easily, but it is in our limitations that God can reveal himself and we can experience his transforming grace and power. A collect in the Book of Common Prayer for the 2nd Sunday in Lent begins, 'Almighty God, who seest that we have no power of ourselves to help ourselves'. St Paul does not link the above scriptural passages with the eucharist, although one eucharistic preface in the Roman mass speaks of how a martyr 'reveals your power shining through human weakness. You choose the weak and make them strong.'

Many ordinary Christians have found in the eucharist the *means* of receiving God's grace and power to overcome and strengthen them in their weakness. It is here that I share my own personal testimony. One reviewer of my previous book *Speaking of Healing*, while describing the book as 'well-balanced and of enormous value to preachers', thought that it was occasionally written in impersonal language. What I have to say next, however, is deeply personal, especially for someone like me who is not noted for baring his soul.

I attend the eucharist every day of my life and have done for many, many years. Why is that? In the words of a hymn-writer, it has become 'life imparting, heavenly manna' for me. I have always thought of myself as a resilient individual with a great capacity for work and hardly a moment's sick leave. After four years in the police in my youth, to try and make a man of me, I entered the priesthood. Before long I had two full-time jobs; indeed, for most of my working life I have run various parishes as well as working in local government, ultimately holding chief officer graded posts. With two children family life has also contributed to a pretty demanding existence, and I have been very fortunate that my wife has been fully involved in my ministry, as well as being a head teacher herself of a church school. But ever since my police officer days I have been dogged by a 'thorn in the flesh'. St Paul asked three times for his thorn to be removed; I must have asked 300 times over the years for mine to be removed. Perhaps, like St Paul, it would be better if I remained silent as to its nature.

When this thorn in the flesh buffeted me I would go into the bathroom and cut my fingers with a razor blade until they bled. Sometimes I would be in there for several hours, while my wife knocked on the door and pleaded with me to come out, but I was unable to stop until the 'attack' subsided. You can imagine how utterly exhausting this was on top of having to cope with two demanding jobs. I would be fine for a few days, then another 'attack' would start and out would come the razor blades, wherever I was (I always carried a packet with me). As the frequency of attacks began to increase I tried every prayer in the book, claimed every promise in the Bible, sought every spiritual empowerment, went to healing conventions, but to no avail. I was in a desperate situation as at that point I had taken on running a second parish as well, together with my demanding full-time secular job.

The hands that had been used in God's healing of others were at the same time destroying me. Sometimes I had to hide my hands from sight so that people wouldn't see the terrible state of my fingers. Even today the trauma of those days means that I use an electric shaver rather than wet shave with a razor.

It was then that I began reading John 6, about Jesus as 'the bread of life'. I had been brought up in an evangelical church where holy communion was celebrated infrequently; I had been taught that it was just a memorial of a past event in which we remembered Jesus' death. It was not, therefore, important to me as a present reality, and after my ordination did not figure large in my ministry. But in my crisis I became transfixed on those words of the Johannine Christ: 'Unless you eat the flesh of the Son of Man and drink his blood, you have no life in you' (John 6.53), and in the Jerusalem Bible translation, 'He who eats me will draw life from me' (John 6.57).

A couple of miles from my parish was a large Roman Catholic church, which 30 years ago had a weekly mass attendance of 14,000; it held four masses each day and ten on Sundays. One day I felt an attack coming on and I rushed down to this church and *in cognito* received holy communion. To my surprise the attack subsided. The same thing happened the next time, and the next and the next. God began to show me that although, as with St Paul, he wasn't going to take away my thorn in the flesh, in the eucharist his grace would be sufficient for me, for his power would be made perfect in weakness; when I was weak he would make me strong. I found out where the mass/eucharist was celebrated daily and at what times, so that should an attack arise I had immediate access to the sacrament, and in my own ministry I began to celebrate the eucharist in church on a more frequent basis.

The problem had always been acute when I went on holiday. We had a cottage in a remote part of the Lincolnshire Wolds and daily eucharists were hard to come by. Our tiny village church was lucky if it had one on a Sunday. I took to driving 25 miles to Lincoln Cathedral for the 8 a.m. holy communion service each day, unless the cathedral had a later one.

One day, however, will always stand out in my memory. I woke up that morning on holiday and felt an attack about to come on. I failed to leave the cottage in time to get to the 8 a.m. eucharist at Lincoln Cathedral, but I knew that fortunately there was a later one that day at 10.30 a.m. I reached Lincoln before this attack took effect and parked the car near the cathedral. It was about ten minutes before the start of the service, but then I couldn't get out of the car. An attack had started; I reached for the razor blades in the glove compartment and began hacking away at my fingers until they bled. I was in a terrible state, and continued cutting my fingers until about 1.30 p.m. when the attack subsided. Utterly drained, I could hardly drive back to the cottage.

When I got home just after 2 p.m. my wife was mowing the front lawn. I pulled up outside and shouted to her: 'Quick, drop everything and come and get in the car with me!' I dared not get out of the car because I felt another attack about to come on. I clung to the steering wheel. My wife climbed into the car (I can't remember whether we had our young children with us as well) and I told her what had happened. We drove aimlessly round the Lincolnshire countryside. I didn't know what to do: we had a friend from London coming to dinner that evening who was staying overnight, and I didn't know whether I would be in a fit enough state to greet him.

At about 4 p.m. we drove into a tiny market town that was miles from anywhere. I saw a Roman Catholic church, and pulled up outside it. I said to my wife, 'I must go in there and pray, but I expect it's locked.' I waited a few minutes, then, just as I was about to get out of the car, a little old lady walked up the church path and went into the church. I said to my wife, 'Damn it. I can't go in there until she comes out.' By 4.20 p.m. she still hadn't come out and by then an attack was about to begin, so I staggered up the path and entered the church.

When I opened the door tears welled up in my eyes. There in front of me was the old lady, all alone in the front pew, and the priest holding up the communion host and saying the invitation to communion, 'This is the Lamb of God who takes away the sin of the world, happy are those who are called to his supper.' And through the tears on entering the church I gave the congregational response with this lady: 'Lord, I am not worthy to receive you, but only say the word and I shall be healed.' I went straight up and received communion at 4.23 p.m. one weekday afternoon in the middle of nowhere.

As I went to sit in a pew I was nearly knocked over by several people who had just come into the church and were rushing up to receive their communion. I thought I was in the middle of a dream. At the end of the service I asked one of the congregation what happened. Very irate, the person replied, 'What happened! What happened! I'll tell you what happened. That silly priest got the time of the mass wrong and must have started it at 4 o'clock instead of 4.30 and we nearly missed our communion.' I was astonished. I had come in, like them, to the end of the communion service, but in fact these people had arrived five minutes early for what should have been a 4.30 service. If the service *had* started at 4.30, had I pulled up outside the church at just after four and got out of the car immediately, the church door may have been locked and I would have gone on my way distraught. Perhaps this little lady had turned up just after we did in order to unlock the church and get it ready for the priest. He may have been a visiting priest which might explain why he got the time wrong. Maybe God in his providence led me to this little town and was also involved in the confusion of the service time, which meant that I received his healing in the sacrament. Who knows?

All I know is that I was in a desperate state when we drove into this town in the back of beyond, on a midweek afternoon at a time when masses are rarely if ever said anywhere, and entered that church to say the words on entry, 'Lord, I am not worthy to receive you but only say the word and I shall be healed.' I received God's healing. The attack did not come back that afternoon and we arrived home to receive our guest, though at dinner I tried to use my knife and fork in such a way that he couldn't see my raw fingers and the congealed blood. Washing up was particularly sore!

Like St Paul, God has never removed my thorn in the flesh, but in the eucharist I have found that his grace is sufficient for me, for his strength is made perfect in my weakness. With St Paul, 'I will boast all the more gladly of my weaknesses, so that the power of Christ may dwell in me' (2 Corinthians 12.9). I remember picking up a little booklet entitled *Living with a Problem you Cannot Solve*. We all live under the illusion that we can solve any problem. But it's when we live with a problem we cannot solve that we are able to experience God's transforming grace and power.

I am aware that what I have said about my need for this sacrament may seem to have reduced it to the level of Popeye and his spinach, or the diabetic and insulin. Critics may also say that this eucharistic healing is really the healing power of the placebo – believing something will make you better *will* make you better. It is the self-healing effect, or the role that religious symbols of hope can play in stimulating relief. Others will point to a stressful lifestyle, and the tension this brings about, as the beginning of this problem. My answer to these explanations is, first, that I thrive on work and am not an anxious or stressed-out kind of person. Indeed, these attacks were worse when on holiday, and hence I always had an aversion to taking time off. Second, I do not believe the eucharist was a placebo for me. If a placebo would have sufficed, it hadn't worked with prayer, or writing out and claiming scriptural promises of healing, and other means that I sought every time an attack came on.

I often wonder what personal religious experience led the nineteenth-century priest Fr Francis Stanfield to write the hymn

'Sweet Sacrament divine' for the service of benediction, particularly these two verses:

Sweet Sacrament of peace,
Dear home of every heart,
Where restless yearnings cease
And sorrows all depart;
There in thine ear all trustfully
We tell our tale of misery:
Sweet Sacrament of peace,
Sweet Sacrament of peace.

Sweet Sacrament of rest,
Ark from the ocean's roar,
Within thy shelter blessed
Soon may we reach the shore;
Save us, for still the tempest raves,
Save, lest we sink beneath the waves:
Sweet Sacrament of rest,
Sweet Sacrament of rest.

I cannot even now sing this hymn without a tear coming to my eye, particularly as the blessed sacrament is processed round the church during a Corpus Christi procession, in a star-spangled throne-like monstrance under a canopy with the incense swirling around it, for I come to this sacrament with a deep, deep gratitude for a God whose grace is sufficient for me and whose strength is made perfect in weakness.

I shared my story with a wise and valued colleague, Chris MacKenna (no relation to Briege McKenna), who is both a priest and a psychotherapist, Director of the St Marylebone Healing and Counselling Centre and chaplain to the Guild of Health. He asked, 'What is going on here?', then answered his own question:

I'm wondering what I would say to sceptical colleagues who will be minded to brand daily communion as an obsessional defence. That would be a possible interpretation, but I'm wondering whether it might feel more right to say that, subjectively, the experience of daily communion feels as if it either keeps something at bay, or that it provides a container within which the self-harming impulse ceases to function in a destructive way? Maybe it's not for nothing that the eucharist revolves around a cut and bleeding figure. Perhaps, within the orbit of the sacrament, our destructive/wayward impulses can be contained/restrained while, at the same time, our capacities for love and growth are nurtured?

Some readers may have found what I have said about 'the bread of life' food that is 'hard to swallow', but for others it will have given them 'food for thought'. A poster displayed on a noticeboard outside the central London church where I was ordained deacon said this:

> The Eucharist is the meeting place of God and man.
> Here the creator meets his creature.
> Here the Saviour welcomes the penitent sinner.
> Here heaven comes down to earth.

Fr Lou Cerulli said: 'If we truly knew and understood what is going on each time the Eucharist is celebrated we would be knocking down the doors of the church to get in.' Professor Porterfield, in her book *Healing in the History of Christianity*, comments: 'The healing power many Christians have experienced in the Eucharist has worked in many ways.'[40] This has been one of them.

## Who comes to daily mass?

I would not want to create the impression that I, or the many Christians throughout the world who receive the eucharist daily, do so only to feed a need to master personal inadequacies. There are many devout Christians who include this discipline in their daily devotional lives to draw closer to our Lord outside of any healing context, for this sacrament augments our union with Christ through the remembrance and proclamation of his death, is an expression of our praise and thanksgiving to God for all his benefits to us, and strengthens and prepares us for service in the world.

However, in the light of what I have said in my own personal testimony, I close this chapter by reprinting here an article entitled 'Who comes to daily Mass?' written several years ago by Fr Ronald Rolheiser in the *Catholic Herald*:

I have been a priest for more than 20 years and one of the great privileges of that has been the opportunity to say Mass daily. At that daily Mass (Eucharist, if you prefer the more contemporary term) I have met an interesting variety of persons. I say 'variety' because there is not just one type of person who comes to daily Mass.

Who does come to daily Mass? In my experience no single category does justice here. On the surface at least, it would seem there is little in common among those who attend daily Mass. It is a most strange mixture of people: some nuns, some unemployed people, a lot of retired women, some retired men, a few young persons, some housewives, and a motley collection of nurses, businessmen, secretaries, and other such professionals on their lunch break. There is no similarity in character among them, but there is something among them (and I am speaking here only of those who truly have the habit of attending daily Mass) that they have in common: in the end, they are all there for the same reason.

What is that reason? It is something that is deeper and less obvious than is immediately evident. Simply put, people who go to Mass daily do so in order to stay alive. They go to Mass because they know that, without Mass, they would fall apart, inflate, become depressed, and be unable to handle their own lives. That is quite a mouth-ful! People go to daily Mass in order to stay alive! I doubt that most people who attend Mass daily would tell you that. More likely they would tell you something to the effect that they go to Mass to pray to God, or to be nurtured and sustained by God, or to touch God and to receive God's blessing upon their day, or because they feel it is only right that they should offer some of their day back to God.

On the surface, those are their reasons. But for anyone who sustains the habit of daily Mass for a long period of time there is a deeper reason, always. Daily Mass is a ritual, a deep powerful one that sustains a person in the same way that the habit of attending an Alcoholics Anonymous AA meeting sustains a man or a woman seeking sobri-ety. I understood that parallel when an alcoholic friend explained to me why he goes regularly to AA meetings. He told me: 'I know, and know for sure, that if I don't go to meetings regularly, I'll begin to drink again. It's funny, the meetings are always the same, the same things get said over and over again. I know everything that will be said. Everyone coming there knows that. And I don't go to those meetings to be a nice person. I go there to stay alive. I go there because, if I don't, I will eventually destroy myself!'

What is true about Alcoholics Anonymous meetings is also true for daily Eucharist. Granted, it is a prayer, it is our primary coming together as Christians, it is Christ's prayer, the perfect prayer that Jesus left us, and it is the place on this earth where God touches us physically. Eucharist is these things. But it is more: it is also a ritual, a container, a sustainer, a coming together which keeps us from falling apart. And we are always falling apart, failing in most everything: we fight, divorce, have relationships go sour, fill with resentment, lie, slander others, fall from grace, betray our friends and convictions, and only have pleasures which are never whole because they are never fully shared. We do not go to daily Mass to escape these things. We do not go so as to fly off into some kind of immortality and freedom. No. The ritual of daily Mass reminds us precisely of the fact that we are unfree, that we are sinners, and that we must die – just as an AA meeting reminds those there of the same thing. One approaches the Eucharist table daily precisely to keep oneself aware of the fact that 'My name is Ron . . . and I'm a sinner!'

Interesting too is the fact that there is something else held in common among those who attend daily Mass: they don't want a service that is too long or too creative. They want a clear ritual, a predictable one and a short one. Because of this, they are often at the mercy of critics who look at this and, simplistically, see nothing other than empty ritual, rote prayer, people going through the mechanics of worship without heart. Nothing could be further from the truth and this type of accusation betrays the misunderstanding of an outsider. Daily Mass is not meant to be an experience of high energy and creativity. It's a ritual act, simple, clear, profound. It's the touching of Someone so as not to fall apart and die.

The response of those who come to daily mass is like the response of those whom Jesus addressed in the synagogue at Capernaum: 'Sir, give us this bread always' (John 6.34). The tragedy is that because of a shortage of priests, the availability of this sacrament continues to be reduced. Hard-pressed priests who may not appreciate its healing power, and laity who likewise may be unaware of its benefits, have contributed to a 'use it or lose it' approach to the provision of weekday celebrations of the eucharist. Perhaps those reading this book may feel encouraged to help reverse this trend.

I was moved to read in Pope Benedict XVI's Apostolic Exhortation *Sacramentum Caritatis* on the eucharist as the source and summit of the Church's life and mission:

At the beginning of the fourth century, Christian worship was still forbidden by the imperial authorities. Some Christians in North Africa, who felt bound to celebrate the Lord's Day, defied the prohibition. They were martyred after declaring that it was not possible for them to live without the Eucharist, the food of the Lord.[41]

# 5

## *Conclusion*

————◆————

### *Sacramental rites*

Years ago there was an anthropologist who went to live with a traditional people, in a far-off part of the world. He shared their life for several years, eating their food, joining in their work, learning their language and participating – as far as he was allowed – in their rituals. Every important moment in their lives was marked by a religious ritual: there were rituals for birth, puberty, marriage, sickness and death; rituals for sowing crops, and for harvesting them; rituals to mark the changing of the seasons and the phases of the moon. Each key moment in their lives had a ritual which connected their daily round to the great story of their tribe, and to their gods.

One day, the anthropologist asked the elders of the tribe: 'What would happen if you ceased to observe your rituals?' The elders were horrified: the idea was unthinkable; but the anthropologist pressed his question. Eventually, one of the elders said, 'We would go mad.' The rituals were important to those people because they gave meaning to their lives. The rituals explained how their little lives – so brief and, from our western point of view, so much at the mercy of disease and natural disaster – nevertheless had an enduring meaning, significance and purpose.

Sacramental rituals play a significant sustaining role in the life of the Christian community. They surround birth, marriage, sickness and death, and include Christian discipleship, leadership, fellowship and conduct.[1] The life of God is imparted in these sacraments through his blessing upon everyday commodities such as bread, wine, water and oil. These sacred signs of God's presence are particularly important when we are at our most vulnerable and the three healing sacraments we have examined play a vital role in imparting Christ's healing and wholeness. The sick and anxious go to the doctor or counsellor today rather than the priest. Yet I hope this book will be an encouragement to many to make use of these sacramental channels of God's healing grace, for the sacramental life involves us in a process of transformation in which we come closer to God through these sacraments.

Some people may have been put off seeking healing from God by the antics of certain faith healers. There can be something about faith healing that actually gets in the way of faith in God, because it is centred upon a charismatic preacher/healer. One such preacher, when asked whether he had the gift of healing, amusingly acknowledged: 'If I had the gift of healing would I look like this?' This is not to deny that many people are encouraged by large healing rallies and that certain Christians do possess spiritual gifts of healing (1 Corinthians 12.9).

Stories of divine healing continue to circulate throughout the world. Healings are experienced in various ways ranging from extraordinary cures, to recoveries more rapid than expected, to those who experience God's sustaining strength in human weakness to help them cope with prolonged suffering. As we have seen, sacramental rites of healing can play an important part in such testimonies.

Bishop Colin Buchanan writes:

> We throw all we can into the battle against ill-health – and not just by instinct, but convinced that God has bidden us fight. In the process we may and often do see inexplicable results (inward or outward) where ordinary calculations of the odds might have suggested nothing but decline . . . [We are] in a battle in which we draw on every

weapon we can, and throw everything appropriate into the attack . . . The full armour of battle includes:

(a) All that the medical profession can give;
(b) straight love, from family and fellowship (and this often has to be costly to be therapeutic);
(c) forgiveness of sins (though not . . . on the grounds that the illness is a tariffed retribution for nameable sin);
(d) the further means of grace – sheer gospel, prayer, laying on of hands, anointing and communion.[2]

## Healing and curing

Even with the most powerful healing ministries the great majority of deaf people remain deaf, blind people remain blind and those in wheelchairs do not rise up and walk. Those who are healed know also that all physical healing is in a sense only temporary. In her novel *The Heartbreaker* Susan Howatch places these words into the mouth of a retired priest attached to her St Benet's Healing Centre:

A complete cure can never be guaranteed, but a healing, an improvement in the quality of life, is always possible. One should think of health as a journey towards a cure, a journey punctuated by healings. And anyway one can argue that a complete cure is never possible because no one can be completely well in mind, body and spirit – such perfection simply doesn't exist in this life. It's the journey towards the cure that's so vital.[3]

The healing sacraments are given to assist us on this journey.

I came across a copy of an old sermon preached by someone many years ago at St Marylebone. It included this passage:

I believe that God is still healing when he is not curing, and an image for one of the ways he does this is 'God the Persian carpet maker'. In the ancient Persian workshops carpets are made on a vertical frame with the workers sitting behind, tying the knots by hand and working to a rough outline. The master of the workshop sits in front of the carpet – directing operations, as it were. When the workers make a mistake or the design just doesn't work out very well, the master doesn't tell them to unpick the carpet, but he works the mistake into the overall design. The final design may not be the same as the one on the rough outline, but because of the skill of the master, it is always beautiful. The back of the carpet is full of knots and broken threads, and that's all the workers can see. But from where the master sits, the carpet is gradually becoming more and more complete. So I think this is one of the ways God acts; not by removing the faults and mistakes in our lives, whether they are 'design faults' (the way we were made), or bad luck, or mistakes of our own making, but by refashioning, redesigning, so that those same faults become part of the finished product. There is a blueprint to follow – and for Christians of course, this is Jesus who, remember, sits at the back of the work amidst all the broken threads and mistakes, encouraging us by his presence and example, while God works away at the final design, incorporating everything into his overall creation and making it good.[4]

The words 'heal' and 'cure' are often used interchangeably. Curing is probably best understood as a successful medical treatment that removes all evidence of a disease or physical condition. Healing on the other hand can have a more spiritual aspect, for the term is often used in conjunction with wholeness. Curing is about the absence of something, whereas healing is about the inclusion or addition of something. Making whole is not a feature of curing, for curing does not make a person whole. Healing and wholeness are more than the physical mending of a broken bone. They involve something taking place at an inner, mental, spiritual or emotional level, such as when one recovers from a bereavement or divorce. Healing can just be about being enabled to cope with an ongoing illness. Even though a disease progresses, healing can still take place regardless of whether or not a physical cure or recovery ever happens, for it is also about inner well-being.

In the story of the ten lepers in Luke 17.11–19 all were cured, but only one was also healed. Nine were relieved of their disease, but their healing was not complete. They went on their way taking their recovery for granted and failing to give thanks or express gratitude, a sure sign of handicapped lives if that dimension is missing, for gratitude is the gateway to growth. Only the Samaritan, when he saw that he was healed, returned to express his gratitude to Jesus, who said to him, 'Go on your way; your faith has made you whole' (Luke 17.19, AV).

## *The acceptance of limitations*

There is a paradox in Christian healing between seeking a miraculous cure on the one hand and a Christ-like acceptance of our suffering on the other. As Porterfield describes this paradox: 'The real genius of Christianity has been to embrace pain and disability and death and not to limit the meaning of health and healing to their expulsion. Thus, many Christians have accepted the onset or persistence of suffering as part of religious life, while also celebrating relief from suffering as a sign of the power and meaning of their faith.'[5]

Wholeness involves the acceptance of limits, for we are all limited in one way or another. Christian healing is the story of how our limitations can be transformed and how our struggles can become the very places where we discover God's strength in our weakness to keep us going, not least through the sacraments of healing. Margaret Spufford wrote:

The acceptance of limitation seems to me one of the most important, and also one of the most dangerous, of disciplines. If you live in a prison cell, it is foolish to spend energy beating yourself into a pulp against the walls; but before accepting those walls, you have to make sure they are there, and you have to make every effort to escape from them. Only the inescapable should be accepted. Everything that can be amended, transformed, healed or ameliorated has to be done first.[6]

This is beautifully expressed in the prayer: 'God, grant me the serenity to accept the things I cannot change, courage to change the things I can, and wisdom to know the difference.' This anonymous poem describes the state of acceptance:

He placed me in a little cage
Away from gardens fair,
But I must sing the sweetest songs
Because He placed me there.
Not beat my wings against the cage
If it's my Maker's will;
But raise my voice to Heaven's gate
And sing the louder still.

One of the mistakes we make is not living with our limitations while we are seeking healing. We are either looking back at what we achieved when we didn't have them and saying 'if only', or we are looking for that miraculous moment when we will be completely healed and set free, so that we can be given some special task to undertake. In so doing we stop living fully in the here and now, by not making the most of the present moment within our limitations. Fr Alexander Elchaninov provides us with an antidote to this state of mind: 'Our continual mistake is that we do not concentrate upon the present day, the actual hour of our life; we live in the past or the future; we are continually expecting the coming of some special moment when our life will unfold itself in its full significance, and we do not notice that life is flowing like water through our fingers.'

Growing old imposes the greatest of limitations. I love the story, whether apocryphal or not, of Margaret Thatcher, when she was Prime Minister, visiting a residential home for the elderly. She said to an old lady who was obviously not aware of who Margaret Thatcher was, 'Do you know who I am?' The old lady replied, 'No dear, but if you ask the nurse over there, she'll tell you.'

The Prophet Muhammad was once asked whether or not remedies for sickness should be sought from medicines rather than spiritual means. He said, 'Yes, you must seek remedy from medicine, because whatever disease God has created in this world, he also created its remedy as well. But there is one disease from which he has not created any remedy, which is old age.'

The elderly don't usually get better. They go on getting slightly worse, every single year, and then they die (though sometimes remarkable healings do take place). As someone said to me, 'Old age isn't for sissies.' People feel a sense of unfairness and outrage that age should attack their bodies just as it had their parents and grandparents. We can no longer look and feel the way we want to and we battle against it. I was sitting next to the late Dame Thora Hird at her 90th birthday tea party given by the Lord Mayor of the City of Westminster, and she said to me, 'You don't stop doing things because you are growing old, because you only grow old if you stop doing things.' But there comes a time when you 'retire' from active retirement as frailty and loss of faculties begin to take over.

George Hacker writes:

> It is when our faculties begin to fail or illness strikes that the real test comes. Here as with ill health at any age we tread a knife edge between fighting our condition and the right kind of acceptance. A positive approach to old age and a refusal to be beaten by its limitations can make a very great difference to a person's whole quality of life, and should certainly be encouraged. However, there comes a

time when certain limitations have to be accepted – to give up driving, for example, or to move into sheltered accommodation. Family and friends need to realise the symbolic nature of these sorts of decisions, and give support to the person concerned as yet another bulwark of their independence is overthrown. However there is a positive side even to this. All the great spiritual writers have much to say about the right kind of acceptance, and in particular of how the stripping of our natural powers can help us to come closer to God and also prepare us for the final stripping at death.[7]

It is one of life's paradoxes that we do not start to live life fully until we have also faced up to death. Indeed life is most real in those moments when we see how fragile it all is. A priest colleague of mine at St Marylebone recently had to watch his wife Rosalind die of cancer while she was only in her late fifties. He described her acceptance of her increasing limitations: 'Eventually the disease caught up with her, but she never looked back and soldiered on, concentrating on the things she *could* do, while gradually surrendering the things she could not.' He found this prayer that she had left behind:

Jesus help me *not* to concentrate on the needs of my weak mortal body, not to make meeting them my aim in life, not to seek self-preservation in this life. By your power make me joyful in my union with you, in doing the things you have prepared for me to do, like you in suffering and resurrection. To forget the past and reach ahead to eternal life with you. You are coming soon! So make me gentle, confident, trusting, thankful, and at peace.

## Beyond sacraments

In this book we have looked at the three sacraments of healing. In the Roman Catholic Church penance, anointing and communion are given as a continuous rite to a person at the end of their life, the so-called 'last rites'. The eucharist is given as viaticum (food for the journey, for the passing over) which strengthens the Christian through death to life, in the sure hope of resurrection, for Jesus said, 'Whoever eats of this bread will live forever' (John 6.51) and 'those who eat my flesh and drink my blood have eternal life, and I will raise them up on the last day' (John 6.54). One of the prayers after communion in viaticum states: 'God of peace, you offer eternal healing to those who believe in you.'

The New Testament promises an end to sickness and suffering. St Paul said, 'I consider that the sufferings of this present time are not worth comparing with the glory about to be revealed to us' (Romans 8.18). The very symbol of Christianity is the symbol of suffering. At its heart the Christian faith focuses on an image of pain and suffering – the cross of Christ. Unfortunately, the great theme of the resurrection of Christ is often left out of our thinking about suffering and death. At a secular funeral there is only one direction to look – backwards to a life now lived. The funeral is literally hope-less, for hope is about the future and the non-believer knows that without God there is no future beyond physical death.

Pope Benedict XVI, commenting on the sacrament of the eucharist, states:

> The eucharistic celebration, in which we proclaim that Christ has died and risen, and will come again, is a pledge of the future glory in which our bodies too will be glorified. Celebrating the memorial of our salvation strengthens our hope in the resurrection of the body and in the possibility of meeting once again, face to face, those who have gone before us marked with the sign of faith.[8]

In 1 Corinthians 15 St Paul speaks about the resurrection of the dead. He uses the illustration of the seed buried in the earth in the autumn, which rots and decomposes and perishes. Yet in the springtime new life appears, such as in the new body of a beautiful flower. In the autumn, if we didn't know what was going to happen – who would believe in the miracle of springtime? So it is with the Christian belief in the resurrection to eternal life. St Paul said what is buried is perishable, what is raised is imperishable. What is sown as a physical body is raised a spiritual body (1 Corinthians 15.42–44).

On the death of my father I tried to explain this to my two little nieces, aged three and five, as we lowered their grandad's remains into the ground. I held up a seed and a flower and explained that the seed or bulb that is buried in the ground will later on receive the new body of a flower. 'That's what it will be like for grandad,' I said. When I got home I said to my wife, 'Weren't you impressed with how I explained that? Did you see their eyes pop out of their heads?' She said, 'Don't be silly, they think grandad's coming back as a flower.'

St Paul speaks also of the creation waiting with eager longing to be set free from its bondage to decay (Romans 8.19–21). In the book of Revelation there are several beautiful pictures of heaven that have become part of the scenery for most Christians when they think about the future. There will be a new heaven and a new earth (Revelation 21.1) in which God will wipe away every tear from our eyes, and death, mourning, crying and pain will be no more (Revelation 21.4). In the very last chapter of the Bible (Revelation 22.1–2) there is a beautiful panorama of this new heaven and earth, where in the middle of the city called the new Jerusalem is the tree of life whose leaves are for the healing of the nations. So St Paul says, 'we do not lose heart. Even though our outer nature is wasting away, our inner nature is being renewed day by day. For this slight momentary affliction is preparing us for an eternal weight of glory beyond all measure, because we look not at what can be seen but at what cannot be seen; for what can be seen is temporary, but what cannot be seen is eternal' (2 Corinthians 4.16–18).

The present sufferings, St Paul tells us, are like birth pangs – suffering that anticipates the coming of new life. He says, 'We know that the whole creation has been groaning in labour pains until now; and not only the creation, but we ourselves' (Romans 8.22–23), as we groan inwardly waiting for the redemption of our bodies. Childbirth and death are both transcendent events. The image of labour pains, birth pangs, is a fitting one with which to conclude, for St Paul likens this world to a mother's womb. If a baby could talk it would probably say that, despite the pangs, it didn't want to leave the comfort of the womb, in the same way that people cling steadfastly to this life for as long as possible.

Henry Nouwen shares this story about a twin sister and brother talking to each other in the womb, with which I draw this book to a close:

> The sister said to the brother, 'I believe that there is life after birth.' Her brother protested vehemently, 'No, no. This is all there is. This is a dark and cosy place, and we have nothing else to do but to cling to the cord that feeds us.' The sister insisted, 'There must be something more than this dark place. There must be something else, a place with light where there is freedom to move.' Still she could not convince her twin brother.
>
> After some silence, the sister said hesitantly, 'I have something else to say, and I'm afraid you won't believe that, either, but I think that there is a mother!' Her brother became furious: 'A mother!' he shouted. 'What are you talking about? I have never seen a mother, and neither have you. Who put that idea in your head? As I told you, this place is all we have. Why do you always want more? This is not such a bad place after all. We have all we need, so let's be content.'
>
> The sister was quite overwhelmed by her brother's response and for a while didn't dare to say anything

more. But she couldn't let go of her thoughts, and since she had only her twin brother to speak to, she finally said, 'Don't you feel these squeezes once in a while? They're quite unpleasant and quite painful.' 'Yes,' he answered. 'What's special about that?' 'Well,' the sister said, 'I think that these squeezes are there to get us ready for another place, much more beautiful than this, where we will see our mother face-to-face. Don't you think that's exciting?'[9]

We have come to the end of our exploration of the sacraments of healing. John Polkinghorne, in an article in *The Tablet* (19 April 2003) entitled 'Destiny beyond death' said: 'One can express the difference between the old and new creations by saying that this world contains sacraments, but *that* world will be wholly sacramental, totally suffused by the divine presence.'

We will not need these sacraments of God's hidden presence in the new creation, for St Paul says, 'then we will see face to face' (1 Corinthians 13.12). St Thomas Aquinas said of the eucharist: 'Grant that I may one day see face to face your beloved Son, whom I now intend to receive under the veil of the sacrament.' The communion hymn ascribed to him says:

O Christ, whom now beneath a veil we see,
May what we thirst for soon our portion be,
To gaze on thee unveiled, and see thy face,
The vision of thy glory and thy grace.

This world contains sacraments through which we experience the healing grace of God, but the world to come will be wholly sacramental, entirely permeated by the presence of God, in which sickness, suffering and death will be no more. 'Beloved, we are God's children now; what we will be has not yet been revealed. What we do know is this: when he is revealed, we will be like him, for we will see him as he is' (1 John 3.2), through eyes in which every tear has been wiped away.

# Notes

## 1 Introduction

1 McManus, J., *The Healing Power of the Sacraments*, Redemptorist Publications, Chawton, Hampshire, 2005, pp. 169–70.
2 Macquarrie, J., *A Guide to the Sacraments*, SCM Press, London, 1997, p. 95.
3 MacNutt, F., *Healing*, Ave Maria Press, Notre Dame, Ind., 1974, p. 275.
4 Morton, M., *Personal Confession Reconsidered*, Grove Books, Nottingham, 1994, p. 14.
5 *A Time to Heal*, a report on the healing ministry for the House of Bishops of the General Synod of the Church of England, Church House Publishing, London, 2000, p. 29.
6 Psalm 45.7, Hebrews 1.9.
7 Cottrell, S., *Sacraments, Wholeness and Evangelism*, Grove Books, Cambridge, 1996, p. 15.
8 *A Time to Heal*, pp. 31–2.
9 Cottrell, *Sacraments, Wholeness and Evangelism*, pp. 15–16.
10 Macquarrie, *A Guide to the Sacraments*, p. 46.

## 2 The sacrament of the anointing of the sick

1 MacNutt, *Healing*, p. 70.
2 MacNutt, F., *The Nearly Perfect Crime*, Chosen Books, Grand Rapids, Mich., 2005, pp. 165–6.
3 Buchanan, C., *Services for Wholeness and Healing*, Grove Books, Cambridge, 2000, p. 22.
4 *Common Worship: Pastoral Services*, Church House Publishing, London, 2000, p. 10.
5 Vatican Council II, *The Constitution on the Sacred Liturgy*, No. 73.
6 *Pastoral Care of the Sick: Rites of Anointing and Viaticum*, Catholic Book Publishing Co., New York, 1983, p. 20.
7 *Pastoral Care of the Sick: Rites of Anointing and Viaticum*, p. 84.

8 Hamel Cooke, C., *Health is for God*, Arthur James, London, 1986, p. 45.
9 *Pastoral Care of the Sick: Rites of Anointing and Viaticum*, p. 85.
10 Headley, C., *The Laying on of Hands and Anointing*, Grove Books, Cambridge, 2002, p. 18.
11 *Ministry to the Sick*, Authorised Alternative Services, Joint Publishers of the ASB, 1983, p. 28.
12 See Macquarrie, *A Guide to the Sacraments*, pp. 38, 47 and 53 for a fuller discussion.
13 McKenna, B., *Miracles Do Happen*, Veritas Publications, Dublin, 1987, p. 53.
14 But see Job 3.20–21.
15 Macquarrie, *A Guide to the Sacraments*, pp. 165–6.

## 3 The sacrament of penance and reconciliation

1 Morton, *Personal Confession Reconsidered*, p. 9.
2 See Dudley, Martin, and Rowell, Geoffrey (eds), *Confession and Absolution*, Liturgical Press, Collegeville, Minn., 1990, p. 58.
3 Morton, *Personal Confession Reconsidered*, p. 12.
4 *The Catechism of the Catholic Church*, Chapman, London, 1994, p. 325 (No. 1446).
5 *The Rite of Penance*, J. Neale, Evesham, 1976, p. 10.
6 *The Rite of Penance*, pp. 4–5.
7 *Common Worship: Christian Initiation*, Church House Publishing, London, 2006, p. 5.
8 *Common Worship: Christian Initiation*, p. 266.
9 *The Rite of Penance*, p. 9.
10 McManus, *The Healing Power of the Sacraments*, pp. 68–9.
11 McManus, *The Healing Power of the Sacraments*, p. 91.
12 MacNutt, *Healing*, pp. 287–8.
13 MacNutt, *Healing*, pp. 252–3.
14 Bonhoeffer, D., *Life Together*, SCM Press, London, 1954, pp. 105–6.
15 Hacker, G., *The Healing Stream*, Darton, Longman and Todd, London, 1998, p. 131.
16 *The Rite of Penance*, p. 7.
17 Baker, J., *How Forgiveness Works*, Grove Books, Nottingham, 1995, p. 8.

18 Morton, *Personal Confession Reconsidered*, p. 14.
19 Colwell, J., *Promise and Penance*, Paternoster, Milton Keynes, 2005, pp. 186–7.
20 Colwell, *Promise and Penance*, p. 77.

## 4 The sacrament of the eucharist

1 Porterfield, A., *Healing in the History of Christianity*, Oxford University Press, New York, 2005, p. 87.
2 Jasper, R. C. D. and Cuming, G. J., *Prayers of the Eucharist*, Liturgical Press, Collegeville, Minn., 1987, p. 60.
3 Porterfield, *Healing in the History of Christianity*, p. 87.
4 Hampsch, J., *The Healing Power of the Eucharist*, St Anthony Messenger Press, Cincinnati, OH, 1999, p. 61.
5 Porterfield, *Healing in the History of Christianity*, p. 88.
6 Danielou, J., Couratin, A. H. and Kent, J., *The Pelican Guide to Modern Theology*, Vol. 2, Penguin Books, Harmondsworth, 1969, p. 227.
7 Crichton, J., *A Short History of the Mass*, Catholic Truth Society, London, 1983, pp. 54–5.
8 Porterfield, *Healing in the History of Christianity*, p. 88.
9 Porterfield, *Healing in the History of Christianity*, p. 88.
10 See Lord, B. and P., *Miracles of the Eucharist*, Vols 1 and 2, Journeys of Faith, Westlake Village, Calif., 1986 and 1994. Also Cruz, J., *Eucharistic Miracles*, Tan Books, Ill., 1987.
11 Porterfield, *Healing in the History of Christianity*, p. 24.
12 See also ARCIC Eucharistic Doctrine, statement 6 and BEM Eucharist 14/15.
13 See ARCIC Eucharistic Doctrine, statement 5 and BEM Eucharist 5/8.
14 *The Catechism of the Catholic Church*, p. 314 (No. 1390).
15 I was not aware of this at the time of encountering my difficulties recorded on pp. 121–5.
16 *The Catechism of the Catholic Church*, pp. 312–13 (Nos. 1384–5).
17 *The Catechism of the Catholic Church*, p. 313 (No. 1385).
18 *The Catechism of the Catholic Church*, p. 323 (No. 1436).
19 *Pastoral Care of the Sick: Rites of Anointing and Viaticum*, p. 58.
20 MacNutt, *Healing*, pp. 291–2.
21 MacNutt, *Healing*, p. 324.

22 Webber, R., *Planning Blended Worship: The Creative Mixture of Old and New*, Abingdon Press, Nashville, Tenn., 1998, p. 136.
23 *The Church's Ministry of Healing: Report of the Archbishops' Commission*, Church Information Board, 1958, p. 54.
24 Israel, Martin, *Healing as Sacrament*, Cowley Publications, Cambridge, Mass., 1985, ch. 7.
25 *The Catechism of the Catholic Church*, p. 338 (No. 1509).
26 *The Catechism of the Catholic Church*, p. 297 (No. 1324).
27 Vatican Council II, *The Constitution on the Sacred Liturgy*, No. 10.
28 Hampsch, *The Healing Power of the Eucharist*, pp. 93–4.
29 Hampsch, *The Healing Power of the Eucharist*, p. 65.
30 Hampsch, *The Healing Power of the Eucharist*, p. 19.
31 Hampsch, *The Healing Power of the Eucharist*, p. 153.
32 McKenna, *Miracles Do Happen*, pp. 59–60.
33 McKenna, *Miracles Do Happen*, p. 60.
34 McKenna, *Miracles Do Happen*, p. 66.
35 McKenna, *Miracles Do Happen*, p. 68.
36 McKenna, *Miracles Do Happen*, p. 113.
37 *The Catechism of the Catholic Church*, pp. 314–15 (No. 1393).
38 *The Catechism of the Catholic Church*, p. 315 (No. 1394).
39 *The Catechism of the Catholic Church*, p. 315 (No. 1395).
40 Porterfield, *Healing in the History of Christianity*, p. 7.
41 Benedict XVI, Apostolic Exhortation *Sacramentum Caritatis*, 2007 (No. 95).

## 5 Conclusion

1 This refers to the Roman Catholic sacraments of baptism, marriage, anointing, confirmation, ordination, communion and penance.
2 Buchanan, C., *Services for Wholeness and Healing*, p. 13.
3 Howatch, S., *The Heartbreaker*, Alfred Knopf, New York, 2004, p. 462.
4 Burden, A., *Images of God*, St Marylebone Papers, 1991, pp. 2–3.
5 Porterfield, *Healing in the History of Christianity*, p. 4.
6 Quoted in *A Time to Heal*, p. 141.
7 Hacker, G., *The Healing Stream*, p. 179.
8 Benedict XVI, *Sacramentum Caritatis* (No. 32).
9 Nouwen, H., *Our Greatest Gift*, HarperCollins, New York, 1994, pp. 19–20.

# BEAUTY AND BROKENNESS
## Compassion and the Kingdom of God

### Martin Lloyd Williams

In this beautifully written volume, Martin Lloyd Williams helps us explore the way we think about the relationship between creation and humanity. As we reflect on their respective beauty and brokenness, we are gently challenged to consider our understanding of compassion, to discern how we may fulfil our vocation as Christians to live truly compassionate lives.

The author uses as a starting point Mantegna's painting *Presentation at the Temple* which is, in many respects, a traditional Madonna and Child composition, except that the infant Jesus seems to be depicted as a child with Down's. It is as though Mantegna is suggesting that Jesus could have chosen to be born with a disability without its affecting the purpose of the incarnation.

How do we respond to this idea? Can we put on one side the notion that Jesus' purpose must primarily be defined in terms of a task to be achieved? If so, Martin Lloyd Williams argues, we might understand creation differently, recognizing instead a creator who recklessly throws himself into his creation because he cannot bear to be apart from it – a God who desires to elicit from us reciprocal love and fierce devotion. And what better way than to come among us than as a person with learning impairments who, in worldly terms, could offer little if any return on the emotional investment we are making?

'I strongly recommend this book, with gratitude and renewed joy in all the riches God has showered upon us through loved ones who live with disability.'                          **The Revd Professor Frances Young, OBE**

ISBN 978 0 281 05858 7

# CREATIVE LOVE IN TOUGH TIMES

## Andrew Clitherow

The problem of evil and suffering is a black hole for many of us. It may seem difficult – even impossible – to pray to a God of love in the presence of so much pain. And the Church is not always helpful. Perhaps, Andrew Clitherow suggests in this prophetic book, it is time to lose the version of Christianity that Western consumerism has produced and to find a new way. Using insights from evolutionary theory, socio-biology and theology, he offers an accessible Christian spirituality which, centred in creative love, becomes a way of life.

'The history of the world is the history of the progress of love at the expense of evil.' In this exhilarating account of love's redeeming power, *Creative Love in Tough Times* urges us to rediscover the Christian faith – and to own it for ourselves.

'Andrew Clitherow's determination to be true to his experience and not to seek refuge in [his] prestigious role has led him to face some of the most intractable and painful obstacles to faith, and to emerge in love with a God whom he discovers in the centre of his own being . . . This book has the capacity to shake the foundations of those who may have grown complacent in their institutionalized security. For many, however, it will have the power to restore hope through its searing honesty and transparent vulnerability.'

**Brian Thorne, Emeritus Professor of Counselling, University of East Anglia and Lay Canon of Norwich Cathedral**

ISBN 978 0 281 05885 3

# WOUNDS THAT HEAL

Theology, imagination and health

### Edited by Jonathan Baxter

In this invigorating volume, a variety of distinguished authors explore the interface between theology and health. Particular emphasis is placed on the role of the imagination within the Christian healing ministry, and how this makes an impact on and challenges current practice.

ROWAN WILLIAMS sets the tone by suggesting that theology is a story about healing, one that demonstrates 'how God transforms flesh . . . by creating living relationships with himself'. ELIZABETH BAXTER reflects upon the healing journey as undertaken at Holy Rood House, Centre for Health and Pastoral Care. MARY GREY draws on her experience of breast cancer to describe what she calls the 'lost dimension' of the Christian healing ministry, 'ecomysticism'. CLIVE BARRETT demonstrates how a Judaeo-Christian understanding of peace is integral to the practice of Christian healing. HADDON WILLMER teases out the difference between forgiveness and healing in order to explore forgiveness 'in itself'. JONATHAN BAXTER, arguing from the perspective of an embodied spirituality, suggests that love, not health, should be the lens through which we interpret illness. ELAINE GRAHAM investigates the question of human identity and what it means to be 'post/human'. GRACE JANTZEN explores the tensional relationship between necrophilia and natality in the anchoritic spirituality of medieval mystical literature. PAUL AVIS reflects upon the Christian healing ministry through the 'indivisible trinity' of beauty, truth and goodness. ELIZABETH STUART, by way of exploring the sacrament of unction, speaks of the 'ever-broken heart of God' and, by analogy, of our own human experiences of suffering, illness and death. BRIAN THORNE, writing from the perspective of a person-centred therapist, develops the notion of 'spiritual intelligence' and its relevance for both secular and Christian healing ministries. JUNE BOYCE-TILLMAN explores the healing and reconciling power of music in our lives. ROGER GRAINGER writes about the role of drama, and specifically drama therapy, as a vehicle for personal and cultural healing. Finally, ANDREW SHANKS, through his translation of Hölderlin's poem 'Patmos', encourages us to face the sickness of our culture and ourselves with renewed verve and imagination.

ISBN 978 0 281 05830 3

# A RAINBOW-COLOURED CROSS

## Personal prayers

### Ruth Etchells

'I don't know what to do, Lord. A lot of the time, I don't know what to do. Situations are rarely clear-cut, relationships are complex, demands are contradictory, choices are blurred. Which way to go? For whom give time – energy – money – attention – even prayer? [And then] you remind me of the simple rule: always to remove myself from the centre of [my] mind-set, heart-set . . . and turn back to the joy of Christ being there instead.'

From *Third Day* • MORNING

*A Rainbow-coloured Cross* will provide comfort and affirmation for those experiencing the pain, struggle, freedom and joy of the Christian life. Richly imaginative, it offers morning and evening prayers for a month and represents the fruit of many years' daily conversation with God. A wide range of Christian writers are featured, including John Bell, Timothy Dudley-Smith, R. S. Thomas, Kathy Galloway, George MacDonald and Dag Hammarskjöld. However, almost all the material has been specially written for this book.

Those of us looking for a deeper spiritual life will be challenged, encouraged, surprised and reassured as we adopt this pattern of daily prayer. Those searching for new seasonal material will appreciate the supplementary section: here may be found prayers which give a wonderfully fresh perspective on Lent, Easter, Ascension Day, Pentecost and Trinity Sunday.

*A Rainbow-coloured Cross* is a companion volume to *Safer than a Known Way*, also published by SPCK. Each book may be read as complete in itself.

ISBN 978 0 281 05786 3

# HOW TO BECOME A SAINT

## A beginner's guide

### Jack Bernard

Those of us who frequently struggle in our lives as Christians may assume there's not much point in striving to become a saint. But as Jack Bernard argues persuasively in this life-enhancing book, we are all good candidates for sainthood because God deals exclusively with hopeless cases! Sainthood is, in fact, God's desire for every believer and available to anyone willing to embark on the journey to holiness.

'Provides a "back to basics" commonsense spirituality, which is much needed during this time of growing polarization among Christians. Sainthood, [Bernard] argues, is sorely misunderstood. It does not require perfection, but rather trust: trust in God and God's will, and trust in the goodness of oneself and others.' **Publishers Weekly**

'Jack Bernard is the last person on earth to think of himself as a saint. This is why *How to Become a Saint* is so refreshing and so instructive. Here is a truly authentic, honest, down-to-earth word on what it means to be wholly undivided toward God. This book is neither a manual nor a manifesto; it is a wellspring of humble, hard-fought wisdom that can be applied by anyone who wants to love God more fully and faithfully.'
**Charles Moore, editor of *Provocations: Spiritual Writings of Kierkegaard* and *Leo Tolstoy: Essential Spiritual Writings***

ISBN 978 0 281 05911 9